A Place in Normandy

Also by Nicholas Kilmer

Man with a Squirrel

Harmony in Flesh and Black

A Place in Normandy

Nicholas Kilmer

An Owl Book

Henry Holt and Company   New York

Henry Holt and Company, Inc.
Publishers since 1866
115 West 18th Street
New York, New York 10011

Henry Holt® is a registered
trademark of Henry Holt and Company, Inc.

Library of Congress Cataloging-in-Publication Data
Kilmer, Nicholas.
A place in Normandy / Nicholas Kilmer.
p.   cm.
1. Kilmer, Nicholas—Homes and haunts—France—
Pont-l'Evêque Region.   2. Pont-l'Evêque Region
(France)—Description and travel.   3. Dwellings—France—
Remodeling.   4. Country life—France—Pont-l'Evêque
Region—Humor.   I. Title.
DC801.P8363P53 1997   96-19315
944′ .22—dc20   CIP

ISBN 0-8050-3930-9
ISBN 0-8050-5532-0 (An Owl Book: pbk.)

Henry Holt books are available for special promotions
and premiums. For details contact: Director, Special Markets.

First Owl Book Edition—1997

Designed by Betty Lew

Printed in the United States of America
All first editions are printed on acid-free paper. ∞

3   5   7   9   10   8   6   4   2
1   3   5   7   9   10   8   6   4   2 (pbk.)

Title page photograph:
The front of the house, 1937. Photo Claude Giraud

For my mother, Frances Frieseke Kilmer.
For Kenton Kilmer, my father, and
Sarah O'Bryan Frieseke, my grandmother,
both of dear and blessed memory.

ACKNOWLEDGMENTS

For their encouragement and warning while I worked on this, I thank Ann Fay, Joann Green, Bill Davis, Harriet Yarmolinsky, Dave Sohn, and Beth Chapin. For aid and assistance, for permission to quote, or for invaluable suggestions and assistance, I thank Jacqueline Block, Freeman Foote, Andrew Heiskell, Ben Martinez, Lowry Burgess, Woody Openo, and Bunny Woodard. For permission to use their photographs, my thanks to Walter Chapin, Harriet Griesinger, Susie Holstrom, Bette Noble, Tom and Dana Perrone. A number of the reproduced photographs that were taken in the 1920s are the work of the Russian emigré whom I can identify only by his first name, Georges; I cannot, therefore, give him the credit that is his due. My unyielding thanks to Bill McGurn for his close reading of the text, and for sage advice which I only occasionally defied.

Special thanks to Mary Norris, my mother-in-law. As her daughter knows all too well, I prefer a *fait accompli*. I hope that now that it is too late for her to protest, she will forgive my quoting from her letters without asking her permission. My only excuse is that I was sure she would refuse. I wish there were more of her letters. Her enthusiasm and the unfailing pleasure she takes in life have been and are among my family's greatest treasures.

Much of this book is the work of my wife, Julia.

"[The last time I saw the Friesekes they had moved to Normandy. There my wife and I lunched with them in their] *damp, moldy, and wholly colorful farmhouse, still reminiscent of an era of tranquility.*"

—Homer Saint-Gaudens, *The American Artist and His Times*

A Place in
Normandy

ONE

We're asking for trouble, aren't we?" I admitted. I'd just hung up the phone after a long talk with our daughter, Maizie, who was holding down the West Coast at the moment and who'd exclaimed, "Dad, I hear you're buying me a farm in Normandy. Great. I'll quit college and take some people over and become one with the land. Lots of my friends are thinking about farming."

It was raining, it was too late in the evening for coherence anyway, and it was also February. Julia and I, at our temporary home of thirty years in Cambridge, Massachusetts, were working on the fight that we had begun in around 1968, which Maizie's call had interrupted. Someone had leaked the status of the fight to Maizie, and she was making what could be the terminal mistake of taking my side in it—as any sensible person would.

"Asking for trouble? Maybe you are," Julia said. Among the failings of mine she has pointed out over the years is my tendency to bite off more than I can see. "An attractive nuisance is what they call it in the law," Julia continued, seizing the opening. She huffed into the Science section of the morning's *New York Times*. I had taken a yellow Hi-liter and marked a paragraph in an article about female circadian rhythms. The author, whom I saw as being on my side of the larger argument, claimed that as the days lengthened into spring, the female, prompted by secretions of melatonin, yearned to fly thousands of miles and then mate. Julia hadn't mentioned the article.

"Wherever you are, there's always an awful lot of extra that nobody knows how to put away," Julia said. "And now we're going to start cleaning up after your ancestors? Supposing we buy this farm in France—where are we going to put it all?" It was not bad for a rhetorical question—but neither of us could answer its obverse, either: *If we don't take it on, then what?*

My mother's mother had always lived with us in America. When she died, she'd surprised everyone with her request that her body be buried in Normandy, near the house in Mesnil, next to the husband she had lost more than a generation before. Aside from some German officers during the war, and refugees as the war ended, and the tenant farmer, the place had been essentially vacant for thirty years. My mother and father, though married in Mesnil, had raised their large family in Virginia, and none of us had set foot on the Normandy property between 1939 and 1966, when my grandmother died. With the disposition of her body according to her instructions, a link was renewed that led the family to begin to use again the house, which my mother had inherited. A number of us began working to make the place habitable—particularly my wife, Julia, and I, with our children. Over the ensuing years we had come to depend on maintaining a foothold in Normandy, and our children had also. Because of its state of ruin and our schedules, we had been able to get to it only during occasional summers. But by the February evening of this discussion, a generation after we'd started working on it, my parents were aging, their children were scattering, and nature was taking its course in Normandy, with less to oppose it every year. Something more definitive had to happen than the status quo, and my solution was to take the place over myself—that is, ourselves—by buying it outright from my mother. This would mean not only that the house would be ours, but also that it would become solely our fault, which had previously been shared among family and humanity, like original sin—which we sometimes referred to as the spirit of the place. Whenever we discussed it, we got closer to acknowledging what it seemed to me we had to do, and that in itself made it progressively harder to get the subject on the table.

Now, on this particular evening of cold February rain, the subject lay (unetherized) upon the kitchen table as Julia kept me company and pointedly ignored the article I'd marked. Jacob, our last child at home, was cornering *Issues of the Twentieth Century* elsewhere in the house by thumping at it on his bull fiddle, imparting fear and trembling to the rest of the building as well; and I, meanwhile, was bottling the apple cider I'd been meaning to transfer from its fermenting carboy since shortly before Christmas. I was up to my ears in froth and empty bottles cadged from friends and brought in earlier this evening from storage in the backyard. Our kitchen smelled like certain aspects of Normandy.

We'd been discussing and avoiding the Normandy undertaking for so many years now that I'd begun to feel I might lose this fight, which I wanted to win if only to resolve the question of whether or not to invest in the new roof we needed for the house in Cambridge. (*Obviously not—we've got the farm in Normandy to pay for.*) We were talking about it but still not getting very far.

Julia, like the cat in Shakespeare's adage, can seldom bring herself to the point of "I will" or "I do" unless there's a churchful of witnesses behind her, a monsignor flanked by priests in front, and no side exits. I pointed this out.

"I normally get by just fine on 'We'll see.' And if your aim is to break bottles, wouldn't it be faster with a hammer?" she volunteered. She shuddered. "I keep thinking of all those empty bottles stacked up behind M. Braye's. How many empty bottles do we need?"

"The time is coming when we'll have to shift from 'we'll see' into either yes or no," I insisted, foiling this attempt at a diversion and tasting the cider. It was thin and sour. My version of the Normans' national drink would still have to sit, its residual colony of yeasts devouring the bottling sugar and exchanging it for gas, for three months in the basement before it might be drinkable (or *buvable*, as the French would say; *imbuvable* is a term used by some in France to characterize persons whom no one can stand to be around).

"Just when I'm thinking that this rain might stop, and let me out into my garden, you want us to head for Normandy again," Julia pleaded. We had long since come to realize that we could not argue sensibly about the issue of the place in Normandy, any more than the Pompeians could about Vesuvius. There it smoked, outside the window: a pleasure to the senses, fertile, and threatening to blow. Maybe. But maybe not for hundreds of years more. And meanwhile there was so much to be said for living in Pompeii. . . .

It would have been one thing to start fresh with an old house. But the task we would face if we bought the Normandy property was worse than that. The old house was hardly new to us. Here, as we knew from long experience, the moment you glanced away from a chimney that needed fixing, something else unexpected would occupy your full attention—a broken crock in the downstairs kitchen, maybe, whose other part you'd seen the day before, in the attic; or an old letter; or Great-aunt Janet's prize for stocking darning. Was that gas you smelled, leaking from the downstairs kitchen, or merely a stopped-up septic tank? Perhaps the worst part was the weight of familial baggage the place contained, even worse than the amount of general decay already completed and the additional ruin well under way. The line of demarcation between septic tank and precious family history was not always easy to distinguish in the shadows.

The thing was, I loved this property, and I therefore wanted to make decisions regarding it that I could not if it remained in its present limbo. Even apart from the question of whether we could afford it (we could not), my project was beset by enemies, some of them, like Maizie, disguised as friends. Julia and I were not people with a large or often even *noticeable* disposable income. If our Cambridge house could use a new roof, perhaps nothing about the structure of the house in Normandy *except* the roof was dependable. (But a roof was, I kept reassuring myself, the most important element of a house. As long as your roof was sound, you were all right.) Our normal life (our *real* life, Julia called it) was in Massachusetts. France, therefore, was the wrong country. The language over there was someone else's. Furthermore, Normandy was dour, as well known within France for its variety of damp as for its apples, cheeses, calvados, or cream. It was cold much of the time, and it rained even more of the time. We did not have to say any of these things aloud, since they'd already been said. So the fight brooded awhile on a plateau of silence.

In the meantime, *But I'm in love*, I could not plead, because I knew Julia was also. If I won this fight, she would lose, in spite of the fact that she had her own real affection for the place. That fondness got confused with her versions of the scars that come from loving any old thing—such as, for example, me—for a long time. We had been married even longer than we had been maintaining our long-distance affair with the house. If we bought into it, I would be expected to take the blame. Both of us knew that was part of the deal.

I filled bottles with cider and set them on the drainboard. We'd been married long enough that our silences and diversionary actions could not help but be part of the discussion. I plinked bottles, and Julia turned the pages of the newspaper. We listened to the rain and did not mention either the circadian rhythms or the roof.

"And every time you used to add on to *this* house to give us elbow room," Julia continued, picking up a line of argument offered to her by the rain, or the article, and building on it, "in case you've forgotten, I'd immediately get pregnant! Every time!"

I checked the boiling bottle caps.

"If we're going to be forever fated with that equation," Julia persisted, "and I have to carry enough infants to fill up all those rooms—well, I'm going to need help. I'll kill you if you even look at me like I'm some youngster with high breasts! Are you ready for the cooperative-nursery-school routine again?"

"It's just an old damned farm," I said, "not midlife off-track sex."

"That place in Normandy is full of ghosts," Julia said. "I don't want to go on about it, but all of them are your relatives. And nice as they may be, not one of them picks up after himself."

Our heads, when we lay in our usual bed in the Normandy house, whether listening for the phone or (when they were younger) for the children, or just hearing the night moving, were used to resting in the corner of my grandparents' library, at the southwest end of the house, on the first floor. Six feet from our bed, outdoors, on the shallow brick staircase running alongside the house between the drive-way and what had been the formal garden, was the spot where my mother and my father, who had established a friendship by correspondence, had first met in the flesh. Beyond that spot lay declining orchard pastures, the ruins of the stable, and the drive, heading precipitously downhill until it disappeared into an unkempt arch of lindens and chestnuts, after which it crossed the brick bridge spanning the stream or *douet* (sometimes called the Douet Margot, and sometimes the Virebec) and met the road linking Mesnil and Fierville.

Walkway outside the library window, 1995. Photo by author

Along this road were people who had been friends and acquaintances and second family of my family for three generations. It wasn't just ghosts; these people were as alive as Julia and I, and we had a place among them if we wanted it.

Suppose, for the sake of argument, that adding our money to our (or at least my) spiritual yearning was not unlike willfully becoming a compulsive gambler, another way to toss time, energy, and treasure—hope and regret—into the welcoming pit of an illusion. Might we not in fairness claim that we could always save ourselves—stop anytime we liked—since all the bewilderment, beauty, and fury we needed to offset the seduction of romance were amply available within these fifty acres of old Norman farm?

"We'll make it practical," I promised. I started capping bottles, looking practical.

"The damn thing's falling apart," Julia said. *Like an old whore who doesn't know when to get in off the street,* she did not say, *but keeps on flagging johns, because she's good at it and there's always a new one coming along. Like you,* she did not say.

I did not mention the allure that lay in maintaining this portion of my family's history. Given that I had nine siblings, who, with their progeny, were all potential visitors to the old place, this was an argument pointed in forty-some directions and all too ready to backfire. I could argue that the past would lose its value if it had no present physical manifestation, and that neither of us would be able to bear to refer to the place only in the past tense. Or I could argue . . .

"I hate to fly," Julia said.

Three holes in the tender place between the tendons on the inside of my right wrist, drilled in by her nails during flights I had taken with her, kept me from forgetting this fact.

By now it was after ten o'clock at night. Jacob's bull fiddle had stopped; the other three children, long out of the house, were now fending for themselves elsewhere. Meanwhile, in the darkness under our library-bedroom window in Normandy, the cows were at this very moment chewing grass soaked with night dew. In another hour, dawn would visit the sky over the hill with cold light, and the birds would stir outdoors and make much of themselves in the hawthorns near the house or in the cover of the apple trees. We'd hear the donkey bray from the next hill to waken Mme. Vera's rooster, and later, as we began our day, the bell for the morning Angelus, rung from the church in Mesnil. Once it was rung by an old friend, now buried within the sound of its voice.

"The problem with you is that you're in love," Julia said. "Suppose it's too much? Suppose this breaks your heart? Hell, who cares if it breaks *your* heart; what if it breaks *mine?*"

Nevertheless—and I truly do not know how this happened— we agreed that I'd go over for several days starting at the end of May, to get a realistic idea of how the land lay. The place had been rented to friends for the end of the summer, and I might as well take this opportunity, so I said, to be sure things would be reasonably safe for our tenants. Since Jacob was in high school still, Julia would stay home with him. That would also keep her honest, she pointed out: she would be tied to the mast while I flirted with the sirens, their subtle bodies glinting through diaphanous garments made of nothing more substantial than windblown sheets of mist, their seductive songs tempting us all onto the rocks of ruin with their promises of green pastures, rushing clouds, and cuckoos.

"You take a look," Julia said. "See what those girls have to say. Meanwhile, maybe I'll steer this boat."

TWO

All the east foreshadows night. Day now belongs only to the western sky, still red with sunset. What more I see of France, before I land, will be in this long twilight of late spring. I nose the *Spirit of St. Louis* lower, while I study the farms and villages—the signs I can't read, the narrow, shop-lined streets, the walled-in barnyards. Fields are well groomed, fertile and peaceful. . . .

People come running out as I skim low over their houses—blue-jeaned peasants, white-aproned wives, children scrambling between them, all bareheaded and looking as though they'd jumped up from the supper table to search for the noise above their roofs.

—Charles Lindbergh, *The Spirit of St. Louis*

On May 21, 1927, at about nine-thirty in the evening, Charles Lindbergh, thirty hours out of New York, after turning southwest at Deauville on the last leg of his flight to Paris, gazed down out of his plane's cockpit. Playing in the pasture below her house in Mesnil, my mother, Frances Frieseke, looked up briefly before continuing her game, which, since she was all of thirteen years old, was as important to her as anything Lindbergh was doing. Now, more than three generations later, my train from Paris followed, but in reverse, the last stretch of Lindbergh's route. At first we crossed, frequently, the stately blue meanders of the Seine. Seeing the barges pondering along the river reminded me of a plan hatched by my godson Gabriel, with whose family I had stayed the previous night: he proposed plotting a beeline from Paris to Le Havre, at the Seine's mouth, and using kayaks to traverse the sewer systems of the towns lying in the river's embracing loops, a scheme that would cut the length of the trip by two thirds. Gabriel has inherited something of his father's approach to complex problems, itself modeled on Alexander's solution to the Gordian knot: it was his father who, at the age of eleven, showed Art Buchwald how to *do* the Louvre in five minutes.

The organization of the countryside out the train window was the same as it had been for hundreds of years—just as Lindbergh had seen it in the gloaming from his plane, and as Julia and I had first gazed on it in 1968, both surprised and delighted to find colors and patterns of landscape that we had seen described in paintings dating from as far back as the fifteenth century. In the flatlands the fields were broad and separated by pollarded hedges. This was wheat-growing country, only recently planted with American corn, or maize. Occasionally I spotted the startling scarlet flash of a pioneer poppy, or yellow fields of mustardlike rape (colza, raised for canola oil); and sometimes the brilliant low blue flickering pondscape of a field of flax.

The train wanted two hours to reach Pont l'Evêque from Paris. Failing a strike or some other act of God, French trains are efficient, comfortable, and precisely on time. I could rely on the fact that a train scheduled to arrive at Evreux at 10:17 would indeed arrive at 10:17. Passengers were informed by loudspeaker that the train would stop for one minute; at 10:18 we would depart as promised.

After Evreux, when the hills started, so did the orchards, in which were frequently pastured the black-and-white native Norman cows. Suzette, a friend of Julia's and mine, an old play-mate of my mother's, and a member of our extended almost family in France, had recently moved from Mesnil to the Loiret and now lamented about the white long-horned cattle that looked into the windows of her rented presbytery. "They are strangers," she said. "I am lonesome for the Norman cows as if they were my sisters."

Whenever I was in Cambridge, I myself always felt lonesome for the scale of the French landscape, which now offered me a reassuring physical comfort as the train raced through it. This being the end of May, spring was well over. The apple orchards had surrendered their blossoms and settled down to reap the consequences of their profligate display. Only a few fruit trees stood out here and there, still in bloom. The farmhouses were surrounded by fences that protected their flowers and kitchen gardens from the cattle. I saw roses, though in less profusion than in Paris; Paris had been awash in roses. The countryside paid more attention to what might be eaten.

The land we were heading into was steep and wet and, once deprived of its woods, good for no large-scale agriculture or hus-bandry other than apple trees, cows, and hay. Although Normandy is slowly changing along with most other parts of the world where farming is in serious decline, many Norman towns and villages are still lapped at their edges by fields and orchards. The landscape out my window remained as it had been (minus the devastations of war) when the allied troops moved through it toward Paris in the late summer following D day, the allied Normandy action that made the name of the province a household word.

My train reached Pont l'Evêque shortly before noon. I had planned my arrival for midday, but not too late—that is, before that phenomenon of provincial paralysis called *le déjeuner* (lunch) began to slam the shutters on all commercial activity. I wanted to shop for essentials before finding out what had happened to the house in my absence. The place in Normandy alone might be responsible for the survival of the future perfect tense in the conditional mood, since I knew from long experience that when I arrived, something might always have gone wrong. The previous year, for example, I had arranged that while I was away, an impossible little bathtub was to be removed from the second-floor *salle d'eau* (bathroom). Resembling the front end of an old VW sedan turned upside down, the tub had to be entered from the narrow end, a feat best attempted by persons with long legs. Once in, however, one had nowhere to put those legs, except around the ears. I had left directions for this fixture to be replaced by a shower.

When I got to the house that year, I found that the tub indeed had been removed from the bathroom, but rather than having vanished entirely, as I had wished, it now sat forlornly in a bedroom, a cast iron memorial to *temps perdu.* Where I had expected a shower cabinet, there was instead a low, square china basin set onto the floor in the place where the tub had been, with bare plaster walls next to it on two sides, and the passage door with its glass pane (which connected to a closet also entered from the billiard room) forming the third side. The project required further elaboration. As Julia might have pointed out, the best directions are not always those administered from afar. As to the offending tub, it remained in the bedroom until one afternoon when I was entertaining a prospective client over tea in the garden, during which collation it was carried away by a small parade of jocular apprentice plumbers.

I was prepared for cold and wet, but when I arrived in Pont l'Evêque, I found that the day was hot and offered a mild, dry wind—unusual for Normandy, especially this early in the season. Fresh from the train, I left my bags with the *chef de gare,* promising to pick them up once I had my car, and walked through the town.

School would be in session for another two months, and the summer's tourism had not yet begun to swell the population, which in winter was between three and four thousand souls. A sort of expanded version of a small French country town, Pont l'Evêque is arrayed principally along a main street that points between Rouen and Caen, with outriding elements springing up along two perpendicular cross streets both descended from Roman roads, one on each side of the River Touques. Under its bunting of flags—all the European Union countries' banners, stretched repeatedly across the main street, as if this were a used-car lot—a few men were fishing from the town's bridges.

My walk through Pont l'Evêque was really more of a skulk, since I did not want the Citroën *garagiste* to see me patronizing the rival Renault dealer (the French word for rival is *collègue*), where, if he had received my fax, M. Fruchon had already arranged to let me have the smallest, cheapest, reddest, and most battered rental available. My parents still kept a car in Normandy, but I wanted no part of driving it. An ancient spherical Citroën *familiale* purchased used in 1968, it evoked hoots of appreciation whenever it was seen floundering between the hedgerows. The Citroën had problems with both brakes and power, especially while driving (and/or suddenly coasting) down-hill, when the ignition cable would occasionally part company with the battery. In spite of its habits, Julia and my mother, up till our last joint stay, ten years before, had never hesitated to drive the car—perhaps because its behavior coincided so well with their worldviews. I myself was scared to death of driving it, probably for the same reason. (My father had no opinion; he did not drive at all, on account of a solemn oath my mother had made to his mother in 1937.)

I had to be quick. Small groups of clean children were already being herded across the streets of the town on their way home for lunch; had I been twenty minutes later, M. Fruchon, too, would have left for his midday meal, and his office would have remained smug for the next hour while I cooled my heels. But I was *not* twenty minutes later, because I had been riding a French train.

I signed for my car and committed another act of treachery against the old hearth gods by disregarding the purists' approved manner of shopping, which requires fifteen stops, and negotiations with thirty people, to secure eleven items at the small, specialized shops in town. Instead I bought what I needed all in one lump, at the Intermarché in the *zone industrielle* tacked on to the Rouen end of Pont l'Evêque. The Intermarché is a large hangar in which one can buy almost anything, using a metal cart rented with a ten-franc piece. I sailed with confidence along the aisles, past fish and fruits and canned goods, hardware and bottles, dodging out-of-breath housewives in need of a last ingredient, and feeling like Art Buchwald in the Louvre. I had my shopping done in the fifteen minutes available before they locked their doors, on which leftover placards from the D-day fiftieth-anniversary celebration proclaimed *Welcome Our Liberators.*

THREE

The Pays d'Auge is best known for its fat green pastureland, apples, cattle, and cheese, as well as its hamlets and its isolated farms. "Mesnil? I know it," a taxi driver told me once. "A place almost completely *enfoncé* [sunken away] *dans la nature.*"

Between Pont l'Evêque and Mesnil, the land was indeed fat and green, though the day itself was unusually warm and dry. I opened the Renault's window as I drove to let the warm wind blow in lungfuls of deep grassy air. The hills rose abruptly on either side of the Touques Valley in soft, weathered humps. Almost nobody else was on the road, and all those I did encounter were in a hurry to get home to lunch. The countryside was defined by ancient hedgerows, between which the smaller roads and trails used by the Celts before the Romans came were worn down to a level five feet lower than that of the adjoining fields. The pastures on the hills, despite the day's warmth and unaccustomed sunshine, were wet and luscious; the cows grazed placidly in their orchards. This mixed use, a hallmark of the Norman style, keeps the grass under the apple trees from going to waste while the apples mature. Cider above and milk below.

I passed through the center of the *commune* of Mesnil, population 100: the church and graveyard, the café, and the vicarage, abandoned by the church (which no longer had a pastor) and now inhabited by English civilians. Mesnil's château was invisible at the end of its long, wide alley of carefully pruned trees, behind a well-kept park. Apart from the church, Mesnil itself was no more than a corner spread of little houses in brick, flint, and half-timber, some thatched, some roofed in slate, most of them built right against the street. Turning at the café, I was held up by a roadful of cows, changing pasture at a pace that would not excite anyone's milk. Behind them ambled a broad woman in working blue who encouraged them by calling out their names and waving a wand of hazel still tipped with leaves. The smell of

The town of Mesnil, 1988. Photo Walter Chapin

the herd embraced me. I shifted down and followed the cows until their road veered into the Bouquerels' field.

Then it was downhill along the narrow road, five feet wide at best, worn pink between the hedgerows. It kept to the broad trough cut by the *douet,* next to the marshy banks hidden behind pollarded trees and thickets of brambles. Before long I came to a particularly overgrown hedge that ran along the foot of the hillside on which the farm was situated. Behind these hedges, out of sight, was what was left of the farm. I slowed and pulled in at the drive, climbed out of the car to open the gate, and stood transfixed by the rich shock of the smell of cuttings tossed over the gate into the drive from the grass trimmed for our nearest neighbors, the de Longprés, Parisians whose grouping of half-timbered cottages was shuttered. Having houses on both sides, the de Longprés control the road at the foot of my hill and could, if they wanted, stretch a chain across it and collect tolls from travelers—perhaps as many as three a day. Their properties blossomed for all that the owners were not in residence, and their gardens were in trim and coyly disciplined. I stood at the bottom of the driveway, the steep orchard behind me, on the far side of the road, rising to the woods that crowned the hill opposite the farm. I heard the *douet* chattering along under the bridge—that was all right—and smelled cows I could not see, looked in my mailbox (new last year and, I congratulated myself, still existing) and pulled from it a damp flier for an electronics shop in Lisieux. I noticed how thick and tall the nettles and brambles already were behind the gate and along the driveway as it started uphill. I glanced toward the spot where the shade of the tall trees meeting over it formed a cool bank. The house I wanted was still out of sight.

Even the foot of the driveway offered the comfortable fit of an old shoe. The hot air stirred and made me dizzy with rich scents. I smelled familiar mud and turned left to face the marshy stretch of pasture between the *douet* and the road, across which lay some of the poplars that were supposed to line the stream. This was Julia's favorite part of the farm, since it was level and she was from the Midwest. She sometimes said she would like to build a house there, in what she called, out of nostalgia for Illinois, "the flat." Everything in view was either dead or overgrown or a mixture of the two, since even downed poplars that anyone would have been obliged to acknowledge had died now thrust up green branches and refused to give in. The genius of the Norman climate normally does not allow, except in dense shade, a square inch of empty dirt. Something grew everywhere. The hair and draperies of the sirens were so unkempt that I could almost hear Julia saying, *Oh, God, it's such a mess*—meaning, *It's so beautiful. If teenagers are going to be so absurdly lovely, why do they have to do this to their bedrooms?*

I drove my car in and closed the gate behind me. The drive rose at an angle that varied between ten and fifteen degrees after crossing the beckoning *douet*. (*Douet* is the Norman variant of the French *doigt*, or "finger.") The ascent began in a splurge of crushed mint under the car's tires. Offering something like a kilometer of uphill going that started in the primordial damp under the alley of lindens and chestnuts, the drive was sometimes more a streambed than a proper road. As my Renault undertook the steepest and most rutted part of the climb, I tried to calculate the number of truckloads of gravel that, if all this were to become my fault, I would need to order to fill the crevasses. The car struggled out of the rocky tunnel of wet shade, and we were in the open, on an old cart track overgrown with grass and a low, blooming member of the daisy family that was

The top of the drive, ca. 1930, M. Braye's house on right.

or was not chamomile, depending on whom one asked. It would take several days of my using the driveway for the plants to wear down to something like a gravel surface. Since the weather was unnaturally dry, it was no problem: the leaves provided traction.

I passed between the arthritic apple orchards that we rented out as pasture and saw the house for the first time, two thirds of the way up the hill, its slate-covered southwest end all black, gapped, and dusted with lichen. Even with its shutters closed, it was a sight that never failed to delight me and fill me with the adolescent yearning that makes more sensible men of mature years run after starlets. The house I wanted stood as it always had and always should, a lady between her two half-timbered handmaids, outriding cottages, adrift in orchard pasture and haunted by woodland.

Although there was less in the way of buildings now than there had once been, this was essentially the same scene that my grandparents had first looked over in 1919, when they came by horse cart from the other end of the long loop of driveway, fording the *douet* rather than crossing the bridge. That slope was easier on the horses. They entered the property through a gate between a pair of poplars pollarded by storms, which my grandfather and old M. Lafontaine, who owned the next field (and much else in the area) used to converse under, congratulating each other on the fact that their boundary marker was destined to outlive them. Those poplars embraced in their ancient coupling at the far end of the plateau cut by the roadway in the hill's face, along which most of the farm's buildings (many of them now long gone) had been clustered. The track passed directly through the busy courtyard in front of Mme. Vera's *chaumière*, whose thatch (*chaume*) we had renewed in 1968. What had moved my grandparents, in 1919, to take on so much? Frederick Frieseke was a town boy from Owosso, Michigan, where his family made bricks. His ambition to control the physical world encompassed canvas and paint, books, trout, and billiards. Something of a dandy, he was neither a farmer nor a manager by temperament. My grandmother, by contrast, was familiar with farms on account of her family's having had a place in Radnor, Pennsylvania (and through additional time spent in New Mexico, on horseback), and nobody who knew her could ever have accused her of not being a manager. I imagine the bargain they struck was that Fred would paint and fish and read, and Sadie would oversee the property, make sure the paintings were sold, and supervise the extensive gardens that she immediately began to lay out, of which now only hints of the boundaries remained.

Frederick Frieseke had arrived in Paris in 1897, when he was twenty-three. Sarah O'Bryan, whom he would marry, came from Philadelphia to Paris at about the same time in the company of a sister and her parents, her father having chosen Paris for his retirement. Counted a painter of some significance during his own lifetime, my grandfather had been forgotten by the time my grandmother died, and it was only within the past twenty years that his reputation had been revived, as a member of the group referred to by current art historians as the American Impressionists. The study of art, and the career that followed, took Frieseke to Paris and kept him there, but it was another pursuit that led the Friesekes to settle in Normandy. The River Epte, in the environs of Giverny, where he, like many American painters had summered, was overfished, and Guillaume Pinchon, a fellow painter and fisherman, recommended as an alternative the Normandy rivers the Calonne, the Touques, and the Risle. Pinchon found a place for his own family in Les Authieux, near Pont l'Evêque, at the end of 1918, after the end of the First World War. Not far away, in Mesnil, the Friesekes, following his lead, purchased a dilapidated farm in 1919 and began to make it theirs, gradually adding such modern frivolities as plumbing and a kitchen. Later, after the stock-market crash, and when they had reached a certain age, they would give up their Paris apartment, and the place in Normandy would become their sole residence. Frieseke had started to enjoy some critical success in the world before the war, and his pictures had begun to sell. In 1919, he was forty-five, and his only daughter five years old; the family of three was apparently in an expanding mode that must have been enhanced by the euphoria of the war's end. It was not that they were going back to the land, exactly, since they had every intention of keeping the Paris apartment on the Rue du Cherche Midi for the months from November through March. And besides, the actual farming of the property would continue to be done by a local family that rented the acreage and lived nearby.

FOUR

I parked in the deep, wet grass in the shade of the house, which the sun had not yet crossed. (It took it a long time to get over the hill, and longer still to get over the slate roof.) I reminded myself that I was here on business and must consider the property carefully, in the businesslike way suited to any prospective investor in real estate, instead of gaping like a thirteen-year-old freshman boy finding himself alone with a fabled senior girl, a cheerleader, who happens to be sprawled, somewhat disheveled and tiddly, and whispers to him . . .

It was not just fifty acres and one big house that I had to think about, but three buildings; not only the pastures, orchards, stream, and crown of woodland, but the ruins, and the potential ruins. Before climbing out of the car, I checked the cottages on either side of the main house. The one we sometimes called the guesthouse, which I had first known as M. Braye's house and where Great-aunt Janet had lived during her first recovery from marriage, should be empty now, and it actually did seem to be empty this time. A squatter ensconced there once had taken us two years to remove. From the other cottage, Mme. Vera's, a narrow plume of smoke reached into the warm blue sky, where a few high clouds ambled. This cottage was occupied year-round by Mme. Vera Tonnelier, who had been living on the farm since the thirties, when she came from Poland intending to earn enough to take home as a dowry by working as housemaid for my grandparents, as her elder sister had done before her. Instead, the war intervened, and she married a local farmer and remained in Normandy (a widow now, accompanied by an embarrassment of goats, chickens, ducks, and so on), the property's most predictable resident. She and her late husband, both ferociously loyal to the Friesekes, had supervised as best they could the protection of the latter's possessions during the occupation. I did not see Mme. Vera anywhere about at the moment, so I would wait to say hello.

I got out of the car and was greeted by the tribe of wood doves that made a continual activity of Grecian tragic-choral moaning from their nests in the eaves thirty feet above the driveway. I stretched, looked out over the land, and smelled the grass, and Mme. Vera's smoke, before I addressed the house that the wood doves were warning me about. I noted the ragged string of goats crossing below the ruin of the cider press fifty feet down the hill, in a sweep of pasture where a few trees bloomed late, their cover of white blossom perhaps indicating that they were about to die. Some of the older apple trees were rotund with a waxy green that was in fact illusory, being mistletoe rather than leaves and set fruit. A pair of hawks wheeled overhead, calling to startle the songbirds sheltering below them in the hawthorn thickets and make them, in panic, break for better cover.

"How old is the house?" people sometimes asked, and I could

The back of the house with wedding party of Frances Frieseke and Kenton Kilmer, June 2, 1937.

never tell them. My mother, who had been known to see things, swore that one summer when masons were doing emergency work on the mortar facing of the southeast corner (that is, the side cut into the hill), she saw the date 1493 carved into a stone, which was subsequently covered in cement. That was the far side of the house, against the garden. This side, above its masonry first floor along the driveway, was faced with slate still damp with the previous night's dew—and it was anyone's guess what might be going on under the slate.

Whatever the building's age, the probable logic of its architectural history suggested that originally it had only two floors—one carved into the earth of the hillside, used for stables and storage, and the other, above it, providing living quarters (five rooms end to end, each roughly eighteen feet per side), topped by a thatched roof. Some time later, the first roof was removed, a second floor and attic were built up from the original walls, and a new roof was added, thatched to begin with but later redone in thin black slates.

The result is large and solid enough to seem to defy structural change. The effect is of a long shoebox set into an orchard-covered slope, with the earth arriving at a level that becomes garden on the side facing the rise, then continuing upward in terraces. Since the earth does not freeze or heave in winter, there is no foundation. The house, all three stories of it plus an attic in which a person can walk upright, simply sits on a terrace of earth. The lower story is stone, with double walls three feet thick—faced with flint but filled with rubble—that support the standard Norman half-timbered construction of the upper floors. Because the house was large and suitable timbers were scarce, the straight trunk lengths were reserved for use as rafters. The *colombages* that serve as wall studs display the erratic shapes produced by branches and are up to eight inches thick, while the arched wooden ribs supporting the roof were once ships' timbers. The intervals between *colombages* are filled with *torchis*, a mixture of clay and cow manure reinforced by horsehair.

"That house is made of mud," Julia liked to point out. *And cow shit,* she did not need to add. *Not even the least practical of the three pigs tried to build with cow shit.*

Inside, the floors are made of the same materials, but with the addition of thick cemented tiles eight inches square and of a warm rose color. Called *pavé normand,* one of the local cheeses is named after these tiles on account of its no-nonsense shape. In all, the house has twelve habitable rooms in which something can go wrong, as well as the attic, which stretches the full length and width of the house and is big enough to sleep forty to sixty refugees, and the storerooms and furnace room on the first level. These last open onto the west side, along the driveway, while the rooms on the next level all open east, onto the garden.

The house is, as I've said, half-timbered, but one would not know it just by looking at it, the building having succumbed to trompe l'oeil owing to the efforts of a previous owner, an architect mayor of Mesnil, Isidor Mesnier, who made the place over in the early nineteenth century. It was in his wife's dowry. What Honorine Bréard brought with her to the marriage was a large farmhouse with the protective coloration of the Norman cow. She and her husband covered its weather sides (south and west) with slate, and its less exposed faces with mortar grooved to resemble dressed stone. They would have entered their house from the formal, garden side, the next level up.

Now, however, of the five garden doors, not one still had a key. When the house was properly closed, only the downstairs kitchen door, opening from the driveway, allowed access. On awkward occasions in the past when, due to my faulty advance communication, M. Joffroy, the manager, had not left a spare key as expected, I had been forced to contemplate breaking in, in rain or darkness or both, sometimes alone, sometimes accompanied by friends or exhausted family; but something or other had always saved me. I had now learned to carry my own key to the kitchen door. The lock was of so antique a make that the key could not be reproduced locally; when I tried once, the wise old men who lived in the hardware store in Pont l'Evêque looked at my original, shook their heads, shrugged, and said despondently, in words paraphrasing those of every preceding generation of wise old men that ever lived, "Ah, in those days they made things differently; they made things to last. It is not that way now. You will find no one with blanks to make a duplicate. Try M. Patte in the *zone industrielle*, but he will not be able to help you." (This prediction proved to be correct, though the attempt made for an interesting day.) But one afternoon, while I was looking for something else, I found a spare key hidden in the attic, and I appropriated it to take with me back and forth across the Atlantic. At the back of my mind was the thought that if I should ever lose the house, I'd at least have the key and be like my friend Saïd, the Moroccan architect who treasures the key to *his* family's place in Granada, which was confiscated when the infidels were driven out of Spain in 1492.

I unloaded the car, stood in the grass, and commended myself that so far things had gone well. I'd arrived in time to shop; there was a good deal of day left; the house was where I had expected to find it; and I had my key. It remained only for me to open as much of the house as I would need. I would use no more than a couple of rooms, so there was no reason to open all the shutters—a couple dozen pairs of them—or all the rooms. I'd be all right as long as the place had been cleaned: the wilderness of spiderwebs, dust, mold, rats, and dead birds that could accumulate over eight months of autumn and winter could be discouraging on first sight, even to a man in love.

But clean or not, this place could, I recognized for the first time, really become not generally ours but ours *specifically:* the fields, the doves, the big wooden Dutch kitchen door, and whatever was waiting inside. I maneuvered the key, and it was either I or the house turning over once, twice, until the door could be shoved inward across cold brick and into darkness fragrant with abandon.

FIVE

When I opened the door, the smell of the empty house seemed to tumble out, along with the underground darkness. It was neither exactly derelict nor exactly clean. This downstairs kitchen, along with its annex, the laundry, was the only room on this level that communicated with the upstairs. When my grandparents first took the house, in 1919, these quarters had long been assigned to the making of cheese. Finding it hard to exist upstairs from and upwind of that operation, the Friesekes banished the cheese-making and installed a kitchen here instead. The dormant microbes could still turn any raw milk inadvertently left out: they lay in wait in walls and rafters, and the entering nose sensed their history, as well as that of the years when the house had been lighted only by kerosene. My painter grandfather did not permit electric light. Beyond all this, the prevailing smells inside were underground limestone, wood smoke, and damp.

Because the kitchen was set into the hill, its back wall was underground. Only a tiny window at the top allowed daylight to enter. Its floor was always forty degrees Fahrenheit, and the ambience was inevitably damp: perfect for cheese molds, as Julia reminded me, adding that we ourselves were pretending to be human life forms. A generation ago, trying to cheer this room up, Julia and I had in the spirit of the sixties painted the walls in a variety of primary colors, which had been slowly crumbling away ever since we decided that a better solution would be to use the room as little as possible.

The kitchen ceiling, like the ceilings of all the rooms on the next story, was supported on oak beams that had to be propped up by central columns because the cumulative weight of all the fat-tile floors above had made them sag so badly. When the Friesekes bought the house and stripped the tile just from the attic floors,

The back of the house, 1919.

❧

the old beams sighed and sprang upward. They must have plastered all the ceilings then, an improvement undone by war and weather sometime after 1940: ceilings were among the things the house was missing when we started working on it, in 1968.

I stood in the downstairs kitchen. It was, if not what it should be, at least what I expected. The damp was only damp, I found, once the open door had allowed enough light in to replace the darkness I had emptied out. There was no grotesque dirt, and nothing dead. Good. The *femme de ménage* had come. I flipped the main switch and got light: another good sign. I started lugging in my bags and my supplies, setting everything down on the brick kitchen floor.

I'd traveled heavy even though I would be here for only a few days. I needed little clothing since I kept a working supply in the house. However, I was carrying fabrics that Julia had been setting aside, as well as a selection of odds and ends either not available at all in France or available only at exorbitant cost. The manual hedge trimmer, for instance, cost only half as much at my hardware store in Cambridge as it would at a *quincaillerie* in Pont l'Evêque. In terms of weight, the prize in this year's luggage went to a cast iron Cape Cod firelighter that a Cambridge friend had bought at a yard sale: she remembered Julia's mentioning once that my father (who lived in Virginia and had not been to Mesnil for several years) was always looking for one to put in the house in Normandy. The standard Cape Cod firelighter is a vertical brass pot with a hinged top meant to hold kerosene, in which an asbestos knob on a brass wand is soaked; this can be kindled to take the place of brushwood in starting a fire. My father, years ago, had found such a brass pot, but it was minus its asbestos knob-on-wand; the vacant pot had been sitting on the mantelpiece of the horse-sized fireplace upstairs for a dozen years, a sacrificial offering-in-progress to the patron of projects half completed. My firelighter, if complete, was far from chic. It looked more like a beanpot.

As long as I'd had to check baggage anyway, I'd brought rolled canvas and paint as well, those supplies being grievously expensive in France, and hard to find except in large cities. I'd already been relieved of the supplies I'd imported for my friends in Paris. For my godson Gabriel's parents, Madeleine and Tom, I'd brought the best-selling, scandalous biography of Pamela Harriman, our ambassador to France, which was sold out at W. H. Smith's on the Rue de Rivoli, and an industrial-sized jar of Hellmann's real American mayonnaise, which they preferred. For Gabriel himself I had brought Wonder Bread, several compressed loaves of it, to comfort his Parisian exile.

The chores that went with first arriving in the house were so familiar to me that I went at once into my routine. I'd left the place in the hands of tenants the previous summer, people I did not know named O'Banyon—friends of friends who had moved on to Calcutta or São Paulo afterward. Communication between M. Joffroy and my side of the Atlantic was rare, occurring only in emergencies, so I was interested, in fact anxious, to learn what impression the O'Banyons might have made. I plugged in the fridge and checked to make sure that we had spare tanks of propane to fuel the hot-water heater in the downstairs bathroom, but there was nothing else to do down here; I wouldn't use this room. I climbed the kitchen stairs into the weird darkness of the dining room on the first floor.

Since all the shutters were closed, only the dimmest hint of light penetrated the room, even in the midday sun. I picked my way across the tiles, found and recalled the complex of latches on the east side's garden door, and opened the dining room to a

The garden, looking east from the dining room, 1988: Maizie Kilmer, foreground; Kenton and Frances Kilmer. Photo Walter Chapin

ferocious blast of green weed brawling with sunlight, and my first real discouragement.

I'd tried to ask M. Joffroy, the manager, by letter, to send someone to cut back the remains of the garden, but obviously only goats and cows had heard the call. The brick walls and their white painted gates, which were supposed to demarcate the spiritual boundary between garden and wilderness, were leaning or gaping or frankly giving in. Hot noon light fell on the retaining wall to the first terrace, which was in an advanced state of disrepair and looked more like a heap than a wall. I suspected that a cow had wandered too near the edge. A general jumble of rank weed and nettle mounted upward beside the crumbling paths and stairways by which it had once been possible to stroll to the linden alley, now buried in woods and out of sight along the far boundary of the property, at the crest of the hill. The cypress trees on the first terrace, which my mother had been assured were dwarfs, had grown as frantically as everything else in Normandy and now towered over the roof. The small *crottes* of goats and wide testaments of cattle dotted and splattered all the terraces that might be lawns or flower gardens, where ornamental hedges had disappeared under long thickets of grass. The round pond that formed the visual focus of the first terrace had been sucked dry.

Here, on a more formal day, my mother's pet hen had gone crazy when she saw the offspring she had hatched from beneath her follow their native instinct into the pond, thereby declaring themselves ducks despite their nurture. Here, in these gardens, my grandfather had painted in his Panama hat, and sometimes his suit, under an umbrella to keep the glare of sun from burning out all color in his work, while Stellita Stapleton or Mahdah Reddin or his daughter (my mother), Frances, or my grandmother took the sun. Here had been formal gardens, trimmed hedges, and, the next terrace up, the cutting garden—all well fenced by hawthorn hedges to keep out animals. Here the gardeners had worked under my grandmother's supervision. The yew tree, all asprawl now on the first terrace, had been trimmed in those days, and kept clipped in the shape of a basket. Out of these gardens had come primulas; roses for the house; nasturtiums, whose cool leaves lined baskets of peaches and whose peppery blossoms made their way into salads; lavender for the linen closet; columbine; marguerites. . . . All that was gone now, but I could still smell the box, marking its territorial boundaries like a randy February tomcat advertising his wares on our evergreens in Julia's Cambridge garden—a good garden, one of which I was very fond, and which my present affection for a derelict threatened to betray.

Frieseke supervising hen and ducklings, 1924.

Frieseke painting Stellita Stapleton on the first garden terrace, 1924.

S I X

I could not face the wreck of the Norman garden, not first thing, and not this trip. I had only a few days, and my main task at the moment was to make sure the house was habitable. I stumbled out of the garden into the darkness of the house again and crossed the dining room to the west side, prepared to hang on to the casement when I opened those shutters—because on that side of the house, the sky sucks at you, and you'll go flying if you don't watch out. It is the continually disorienting genius of this floor to assault you with burgeoning, rampant green where the rooms open on the garden to the east, whereas the windows on the west want to drag you right out over the valley. That window had a hot blue sky in it today. I left the window open, like the garden door, because the house was cold. Then, too, the damp seemed greater than usual, and I hoped it might burn off if enough of the day outside washed through. Once the doors and shutters were open, the dining room became visible. I knew it well, but it felt odd—not so much clean as smeared. It was now, and must always have been, the most used room in the house, originally the big farm kitchen where meat was roasted on a spit and pots were kept boiling over a constant fire in the fireplace that took up most of the wall between this room and what was now the library. Something was wrong in here that I could not put my finger on. I realized that I was tired, discouraged by the state of the garden, gritty from travel, and disoriented by the change of time as well as by hearing someone *not* saying, in a voice resembling Julia's, *How can we take on this place if you can't even manage to get the garden trimmed?*

Julia had driven me to the plane and seen me off, loquacious with the combined hopes and anxieties that accompany a loved one on a transatlantic flight—a loved one, that is, who has been instructed to buy three hundred thousand dollars' worth of flight insurance. Because of the time difference, it was still too early for me to call and let her know that I'd arrived safe, and to hear her disappointed exclamation of relief that doom this time was coming in an as yet unimagined form. But I did pick up the telephone to make sure there was a dial tone.

Her first words to me in the past, when I was here without her, had always been, "Is it beautiful?" Because, of course, it was—and that was true rain or shine, and whether or not the garden looked like Jacob's room and my studio at their worst, combined, and tramped through by extinct and flightless birds of prey. Outside the west window, over the dining table, the blue air wavered with the sound of birds—not just the relentless chorus of doves, which had already so merged with my expectation that I no longer heard it; but songbirds I could not name darting in the orchard, and a cuckoo, and Mme. Vera's ducks and chickens. Across the road (two hundred feet below, and invisible from here because of the intervening vegetation and the ruin of the cider press), on my level on the opposing hill, half a dozen cows wandered, nosing the edges of a patch of bracken. I heard metal knocking somewhere, sounding like cowbells, but probably only Mme. Vera careening a tin basin; and a tractor trimming the nettles, thistles, and brambles out of a field nearby. This should be done to my fields also—and would be, I told myself, if I were here often enough to cause the farmer renting them to make the place look cared for.

The dining room, looking west across the valley, 1986. Photo Dana Perrone

In spite of the garden, I'm still ahead, I thought. *I'll have a cup of tea and then see to the house.* I found the teakettle where the O'Banyons had hidden it in the upstairs kitchen. Unless we were overwhelmed with guests or family, this was the only kitchen we normally used. It had once been a butler's pantry and was connected to the dining room by a window opening as well as a door.

Julia and I found it easier to get by on two propane burners than to run upstairs and down to use the big, dark, cold, and damp downstairs kitchen—so long as we were neither ambitious in our cooking nor too numerous in our eating.

I took the kettle to the sink to rinse it out and found there was no water. The plumber had not come to get it started. Now I understood the persistent smearing I had noticed in the cleaning job. A *femme de ménage* had come, seen, but not conquered, though she'd done the best she could without water.

I did not try to turn the water on myself. The piping in this big house was a palimpsest and mystery of interconnected pipes, sluices, conduits, valves, and siphons going back to the Cenozoic, and far beyond my comprehension. When, on a mistaken occasion in the past, I once fell back on my American self-reliance, I succeeded only (working by flashlight) in opening the connection to the town supply, underground in the pasture on the far side of the driveway, as well as the main valve in the downstairs kitchen: water began pouring not only from all the faucets that had been opened to drain the system the previous winter, but also from stopcocks located here and there on walls and ceilings throughout the house. I had to turn the whole thing off and spend a wet night of drought before I could make contact with a plumber.

It occurred to me that the electricity had been running long enough to burn out the empty hot-water tank. I went downstairs, shut off the main switch, and was instantly back in 1493 A.D.

I checked my watch. Everyone else in the civilized world (i.e., France) should now be on the waning edge of lunch, replete and somnolent and therefore at my mercy. I telephoned M. Joffroy's, four miles down the road, and apologized to Mme. Joffroy for the interruption.

"Ah," Mme. Joffroy said. I was in France? Good. And I had got into the house this time? Good. There was a problem. Since last winter, the key had been with the plumber, who had given it, as instructed, to the *femme de ménage*, who in turn had disappeared into the countryside. Therefore, what could the plumber do? It was a good thing I had brought my key, and "all is going well with your family?"

Absconding into the countryside with the house key did not sound like the responsible woman I had met last summer, I said.

Ah, but she was not the one. That one had gone. No one knew where she was. It was another one.

The practical voice of conscience, which often sounded like Julia's, whispered something in my ear that I refused to listen to. Instead, I telephoned M. Le Planquay, the plumber. He was at home, at table, and spoken for by Mme. Le Planquay, who had her own explanation for the nonexistence of running water in the house, somewhat different from Mme. Joffroy's but with the same sad ending. But knowing that it was now possible to get inside, she promised to send a *gars tout de suite*.

I followed the plumber's *gars* (workman/stripling) around the house when he came chittering up in the bright-yellow vehicle in which he had been returning from lunch to whatever job he was on. I remembered his car from the previous year, but it now bore a new trophy on its aerial, a woman's frilly garter of the kind Americans fling at wedding receptions. This was the same man who the summer before had transformed the worst end of the useless upstairs passage closet between bathroom and billiard room into a shower, eventually completing the job by laying tiles directly over the closet door, glass panes and all. One of my hopes for the future was that no one would ever attempt to open the door from the other side.

The *gars* and I shook hands and agreed about the weather. He was a young man, though already well seasoned in his trade and out of the apprentice stage, fairly short and stocky, with an inch of cigarette living on the right corner of his bottom lip. He let me watch what he did, both of us recognizing that his livelihood was not at risk: it would take years of apprenticeship before I could do this job myself, even supposing I had any aptitude for it. I might come to own this plumbing, but I would never master it. Starting the water involved running back and forth between the house and two underground valves in the pasture, dashing from the wood room on the northwest end of the ground floor to the furnace room on the southwest end, then to the laundry room, the downstairs kitchen, the upstairs kitchen, and the bathrooms on the first and second floors, then finally to the water heater (again in the furnace room). The house even boasted valves where no one would have thought to look for pipes—a strange feature in a structure in which all the walls were solid, and nothing could be concealed, plumbing and electricity being very recent additions. We had installed the present systems only at the end of the summer of 1968, intending them to serve as a temporary measure.

The *gars*, while stopping this cock and releasing that valve, congratulated me on my not having blown up the hot-water heater. He finished, wished me joy of my water and a long prolongation of the good weather, and chittered back down the driveway in his little yellow car. Now that I had running water, I felt I had abolished the dark ages. Civilization would be assured once I had tea. I put the kettle on.

SEVEN

Our practice, when the house was vacated at the end of summer, was to have the rugs rolled and the curtains folded and put away. Once light was admitted, the rooms had a dejected air, needing more color and feel of habitation than were provided by the paintings of mine I kept on the walls. Until a fire could be lit in the dining-room fireplace, that dependable source of heat and comfort was simply big and black—and all in all, the inside of the house was a grim contrast to the belligerent and fecund wallops of green and sky that shoved against opposite sides of the room, from the door and window into the garden on one side, and from the window overlooking the valley on the other, where the sun would set in about eight hours.

The dining-room ceiling, like those of the other rooms on this floor, was low—about seven and a half feet. The walls were made of plaster grooved to look like laid stone, and had once been painted accordingly; the ceiling, meanwhile, had been allowed to go black with smoke. After we painted everything white or cream, with the woodwork and window casements a subdued but nevertheless defiant yellow, Julia had announced, "It looks less like a tunnel." But having been empty so long, the room seemed derelict now, even when stroked by hot daylight from outside. Rugs could wait, and curtains, but the place must have color as well as light, and some dry air. It demanded color the same way a slow brown meal cries out for salad.

While my tea steeped, I threw one of the cloths that Julia had sent with me across the dining table, which wanted to seat ten serious diners. The cloth had bright-red and white stripes. When I sat down, I realized something was missing. The large round wicker tray that should be tucked into its metal rail along the wall, next to my place at the table, was gone. This one missing thing gave me a sensation of disquiet worse than that occasioned by the lack of running water. We'd never used the tray, but for me it preserved the illusion of that uneasy "era of tranquility" that Homer Saint-Gaudens had written about, which he located within the brackets of the Great Depression on one side and the Second World War on the other. I had photographs of my grandparents having tea with friends, using this tray and seated not twenty feet away from where I now sat. Nobody in these photos was dressed for the countryside—that is, not for field work; everyone wore a suit or a nice dress, and a hat of absurd elegance, for all that the nearest cow flop might be no more than seventeen feet away, on the other side of the white gate. You could almost hear the ancestors of Mme. Vera's chickens gibbering. That era was lost to me, it was true, but at least I'd always had the tray.

That tray belonged here. It was part of the package. Measuring some three feet across, it would be hard for a renter to hide or misplace or carry home in a suitcase. It was above all

Tea outdoors, 1924. (Left to right, Mrs. Hoeveler, Stellita Stapleton, Mrs. Stapleton, Edith Frieseke [Aunt Dithie], Frances Frieseke, Mahdah Reddin, Germaine Pinchon, Mme. Pinchon [seated]).

an emblem of the house, having survived unscathed and unmoved throughout the whole war, being almost the only thing that was still where it should be when we returned in 1968. Back then, my mother had taken its continued presence in the wreck as a good omen; now, its absence prompted in me a nagging awareness of disproportion that made it impossible to sit still for wondering what else was missing or awry. What had the O'Banyons done with the tray? Or had someone else been in here during the winter? I looked around.

Not much in the dining room could be mislaid. The table was so large and square and the floor so uneven that there was only one place in the room that it could go, and even so, when diners were numerous, somebody had to compete with one of the posts that held the ceiling up. The other furniture, aside from the chairs, was similarly cumbersome: a contemporary couch that could become a bed, and one and a half wooden armoires to hold china and necessaries. Against one wall was the masonry side-board on which in the old days dishes could be kept hot over pans of charcoal. Now it housed the telephone.

With all its doors, shutters, and windows open, the dining room had become inhabited by the voices of birds that were not yet aware that anyone was here. A blackbird sang from one of the fruit trees in the garden's second terrace, which was now striving to become woods again. I followed the sound of one of the fat black flies that had no business in the house, but entered by the garden door and paraded directly through its shade in a dis-tracted beeline to pass out the casement window next to me. It buzzed over the absent wicker tray and into the bright trough of the valley, looking for a cow's wet muzzle or dropping to belabor.

That busy industry of flies, like the cries of the wood doves and the scent of box from the garden side of the house, and grass and cows from the other side—if all those were right, nothing else could be that far wrong. As long as I was here, I decided, I would not camp out after all but would allow myself to open the rest of the rooms on this floor, and live at least that civilized.

As I moved through the rooms, I forced myself not to look for the tray, knowing that could lead only to the serendipitous dis-covery of other missing links to lost causes. Instead, I pretended to put the tray out of my mind, along with some of the other, more complex questions I would have to entertain while I was here, such as what to do about the kitchen(s).

Next to the dining room, and south of it, was the library, where I would sleep; then, reading northward from the dining room, the half-kitchen, the salon, and the bath and guest rooms, all of which I resolved to open. The remaining space on this floor, next to the central staircase leading up to the next floor, was taken up by the jam closet, which I would *not* open for as many years as I could put it off.

In my grandparents' day, the library had been a library. There was no bed in it then as there was now, but the same desk sat at the same perpendicular to the window overlooking the driveway; here my grandmother wrote letters and, when she stood, jostled her husband's wicker fishing creel, which hung on one of the room's two supporting posts. Often my grandfather read there while my grandmother sewed or knitted (her generation kept its hands busy). Sitting at that desk to read, an occupation that he favored over painting, my grandfather could see when a visitor came up the driveway, giving him plenty of time to be out the door and into the woods with his book before the knock on the door. He had begun collecting books as a boy in Owosso, buying Horatio Algers from a peddler until his grandmother weaned him onto Dickens's *Oliver Twist*, assuring him it was another rags-to-riches story.

After-dinner coffee might be taken in this room, and sometimes there was a painting in progress here, with my grandmother reading aloud if my mother was posing. The smell of the dining room, reaching into the library, was dominated now by the acrid aura of the former's big damp chimney and its bed of ashes, left behind last fall to foster the initial fire of summer. That staleness I would easily fix tonight by making a fresh fire. I brought my bags up and took possession of the library.

Then I opened the salon, a room elevated by Mayor Isidor Mesnier to this Parisian level from the mere *salle* it would have been in an honest farmhouse. I passed through its circle of variegated chairs, its sifting bouquets of dried flowers, its little ornamental tables giving in, in different ways, to woodworm and gravity. The salon had once been papered with the Bay of Naples; it still felt damp, though the bay itself had washed away after the war. Nothing untoward met my eye on this first glance, except that all felt damper and colder than I remembered. I noticed mold growing on one of my paintings of the *Douet Margot*, which was as close as the salon now got to the Bay of Naples. I threw open the garden door.

After Frances married, in 1937, and moved away ("I didn't think you were that kind of girl," her surprised and dejected father said), my lonesome grandparents had photographs taken of the house to comfort the young bride should she become homesick amid the excitement of her new life. From those photographs, and from paintings that Frieseke did in this room, I was familiar with the formal and rather eccentric nineteenth-century look it had then, of which almost nothing remained now.

I checked that the huge bathroom next to the salon had cold water. At some point in the future I might go outside to instigate its hot water. The toilet's tank, up against the ceiling, chuckled and screamed as it always did when it filled, loudly enough to waken, if not the dead, then at least anyone who inhabited the guest room next door. (That charming little paneled room, the same size as the bathroom, tended, despite its fireplace, to be the dampest room in the house.) The loose tiles in the bathroom floor were no more numerous or looser than I remembered. The permanent spiderweb in the exact center of the cold radiator under the bathroom window overlooking Mme. Vera's was tenanted, as it should be, by this year's large black spider, which, if I killed it, would be replaced by morning by another exactly like

The salon, with Frieseke's portrait of Frances, 1937. Photo Claude Giraud

it—one similar to, but different from, the one that always lived in the bathtub drain.

Hovering just beneath the smell of the fireplace were the symphonic strains of plaster dust and damp and sifting particles of wood digested by the worms in the furniture; the varied dirts of woods and pastures, blown in under the doors; smoke; linen; mothballs when closets were opened; and old books. The house contained as great a volume of books as it did of *torchis*, the material used between the timbering. I had mentioned to Julia once, in our continuing argument, that one good reason for us to take on the ownership of all this was to avoid having to answer the question "If we don't, what are we going to do with all those books?"

Aside from the missing tray, everything was as exactly familiar to me as a loose tooth the nerves and tongue have grown accustomed to. I opened the doors and shutters of each room and looked outside, knowing that when I called Julia, the first thing she would ask was, "Is it beautiful?" Then she would want to know what room I was sleeping in, aware that there were six possibilities—or seven, counting the couch in the dining room. And I would answer, as she knew I would, "The library," because I wanted to be near the telephone in case she called. Anyway, there was no reason to go through the bother of opening the rooms upstairs.

She'd ask how the cloths she'd sent over looked. All but the red-and-white-striped one were still packed. *You know, honey, for someone who's resisting this move, you ought to notice that you're adding to it, not subtracting—making it more to give up if we don't do it,* I mumbled or thought. Since I was alone, it didn't much matter which.

EIGHT

A sound I could not decipher woke me at three in the morning. I struggled into consciousness, thinking how many persons breathe their last at about three A.M. I heard random, prolonged knocking and breaking of china, interspersed by equally random, purposeful, and prolonged silences. I was in the library, as planned, with the door closed between me and the dining room. I lay awake listening, trying to understand the sound before confronting its maker. It could be a person moving in the next room—I could attribute human emotions to the brittle, tentative quality of the sounds of tapping, and of china juddering against adjacent crockery—but the lengthy silences seemed wrong for a human.

The darkness in my room was intense, if incomplete. Because we were quite far north—on the same latitude as Montreal—summer made for long daylight and only a few hours of perfect darkness. Mesnil was far from Le Havre, the nearest city that might put a permanent smudge of light on the horizon. I couldn't claim to see anything. As I studied the sounds, I eliminated banging shutters, since I knew the shutters should be secure; or a casement window left open, which would make a regular whack, often accompanied by the release of glass panes that would shatter on the tiles. I'd closed up everything downstairs before going to bed, but I'd never got to the second floor the previous afternoon, instead allowing myself to be distracted by other things. If the noise was caused by something not fastened upstairs, it had been flapping like that all winter—but no, the sounds that had wakened me were nearby, and they said trespass.

The library, with Mrs. Frieseke, 1937. Photo Claude Giraud

Was it rats? The intruder's movement had a rat's feral quality of alien intent, preying on civilized constraints even while taking advantage of them. But the sounds carried too much force for a rat. They had about the right weight for a cat, but with too much clumsy despair for that animal in its element (which a dark house was). Besides, I could not figure out how a cat would have gained access.

I thought about last year's bees and felt my skin prickle while I listened to the thing moving. During the previous summer, when I had been here for some time alone, the library had been visited regularly by honey bees whose hive I never found, though I thought it might be under the slates of the scalloped overhang (or *auvent*) meant to keep rain from trickling down the outside walls under my windows. In the room above the library, the bees had been more plentiful, but that was easily explained by the presence there of a fireplace, in the cool darkness of whose chimney they liked to congregate and gather carbon in the form of soot for their architecture, wax being carbon in a more translucent organization. That, at least, was my theory about the upstairs bees last summer. I'd thought a lot about bees, and learned somehow that one of the forest *métiers* in Normandy in the 1500s and earlier was that of *bigre*, an itinerant bee-man licensed by the owning class to collect wild swarms in the forest and carry them in wicker baskets to sell to settled people who needed them for their hives. The bees in my library were not even descendants but rather clones of those farmed in that way. Still, that did not exactly explain where they came from. In my library bedroom the fireplace had been filled in with cement to provide a draft for the furnace, and the ceiling was a foot thick (made, like the walls, of timbers interspersed with *torchis*) and tiled on the upper surface. It offered no passage for insects. Even on days that were too damp to leave the windows open (which days had been in the majority), the bees last year nevertheless had arrived in dozens during the course of the morning and afternoon, to mourn angrily against the western window glass as evening dwindled to despair.

I did not believe in ghosts—something of a waste since, as Julia had said, the house must be full of them. In my family, on my father's side, everyone saw ghosts. In my position, in this bed that, actually, he used to occupy, my father would have gone back to sleep at this point, satisfied that the noise was nothing more than a wandering soul in the next room doing the supper dishes left unwashed for morning.

What about the *femme de ménage* who had, according to Mme. Joffroy, disappeared into the countryside with the house key? Someone somewhere had that key. Once in the past, also during the blackest part of the night, I had found that one end of the house was being unexpectedly occupied by another person. I had not given advance warning that I was coming. (It was after that incident that we had asked M. Joffroy to manage the property.) If someone else in the house had chosen this moment to make a furtive exit, I thought, I should not interfere. But I was curious, and the noises continued until I finally decided to have a look.

I knew the house well enough to move through it barefoot in the dark, taking my direction from the promptings of sense memory and a certain dent in my skull. Most of the doorways in the house did not anticipate my height, but I wore my dent with Lamarckian pride since my rangy grandmother had had one just like it. In the passage between dining room and salon, the less-than-six-foot-tall doorway was further articulated by a step that coincided with the opening. The simultaneous step up and an insufficient last-minute bob were what had caused the transverse dent in the top of my grandmother's head, and then later in mine. I might be a slow study, but now almost the first thing I did when I arrived in France was duck.

Something crashed. I opened the heavy paneled door from the library into the dining room and saw a white blur tilting at a corner shelf almost at ceiling level, near the stairs, from which my father's part-of-a-brass-Cape-Cod-firelighter had just fallen (I'd moved it to give pride of place to my own beanpot) and where something else now chattered in a breakable way. Above it, the blur was resolving itself into feathers and a large owl's frantic puzzlement. The bird was trying to perch on a pair of glass candlesticks, its exposed underside glowing like dusty moonlight. I realized that my eyes were accommodating to the darkness, which must be, after all, less than absolute. Pale moonlight, interrupted by heavy cloud when I woke, was now entering the windows. The owl shoved off from its perch, thereby also shoving off the perch itself, which shattered on the floor as the bird careened from the dining room into the salon.

The salon into which my avian visitor had flown had, in its day, been filled with music, and I was pleased that the friends who were to rent the place later in the summer were musicians. The house had once boasted two pianos: my mother's, in her bedroom over the library (where the bees gathered sometimes), and another here. Everyone in the family had music. My grandfather was a disappointed tenor whose maturing into the range of baritone had forced him to renounce his hopes for the operatic stage and take up painting. My grandmother Sadie, at the time she met him in Paris, was studying the cello, and she played the piano as well. My mother, Frances, was for her part a serious student of the latter instrument, a pupil of Albert Levêque in Paris.

In September of 1897 Freddy, at twenty-three, had played the guitar and sung during his first Atlantic crossing, on the S.S. *Massachusetts,* a cattle ship with a cargo of "three hundred and eighty cattle, two hundred and sixty four horses and twenty three missionaries; and the missionaries are quite as quiet as the cattle, and the cattle fully as quiet as the missionaries." He was on his way to fame and fortune, or at least Paris, in the company of Will Howe Foote, another aspiring painter from Michigan, who recorded the voyage in his diary. Another entry read:

> The evening was grand. Officers played their mandolins and Frieseke, Baxter [another passenger] and the "can't-lose-me" girl in the white slippers and I sang all the songs we knew and then we three boys drew our steamer chairs to the rail and watched the moon and dreamed.*

Frieseke sang in Paris at the studio gatherings of friends; and he sang at the easel in the Académie Julian in the early days; and he sang at his easel in Mesnil (so long as things were going well).

The salon was, in a way, still filled with music, though its piano was gone. (Two keyboards were gradually giving up their ivory and their ebony in the *cave* downstairs, a project begun by one of my children; the rest of the instruments had no doubt been consumed in the course of the terrible cold that drove the refugees to burn much of the furniture while they crowded here during the war.) But there were still, in the salon, heaps of sheet music, from hymns to be used in the church of Notre Dame du

*From the diary of Will Howe Foote, in the collection of his son, Freeman Foote.

The salon, 1995. Photo by author

Mesnil, to Bach or Schubert duets, to Chopin polonaises, to the newest and hottest popular best-sellers of the 1920s: "The Cootie Tickle (Over Here It's the Shimmie Dance)"; "The Gum Chewer's Song"; "Mon Petit" ("Sonny Boy" translated into French); "Softly, as in a Morning Sunrise"; "A Kiss in the Dark"; "Lover Come Back to Me." Someone played and sang all those songs in this room.

The owl was too terrified to make music, or even its usual utterance. I did not follow it into the salon, not wanting to worry it more. The door to the stairs was closed, which meant that the owl must have stooped through the chimney and been unable to negotiate the return trip. Hearing decorative breakables start to teeter and topple in the salon, I opened the window over the dining table; through it the freedom of the chill night air beckoned. Then I opened the door to the garden on the opposite side, flooding the room with night wilderness and as much damp as had blown off during the afternoon.

Rather than trying to herd the owl from the salon into the dining room again, I stepped back into the library, closed the door, and waited, sitting at my desk by the window and looking out at the fields and orchards in their thin wash of moonlight. I listened for what should be the soundless passage of the bird once it found its way clear into the open fields, which glowed now with a cold skin of dew. For the first time it occurred to me that I was alone. As much as I enjoyed solitude, I was inclined to wreck it by filling it with work, forgetting that solitude was supposed to lead to the consolation of philosophy. Moonlight and solitude together should inspire at least reverie—but I could not get past that gnawing feeling of contentment that took up the space discomfort would otherwise have filled with productiveness or at least noticeable musing.

Some places are innately beautiful, and this was one of them. Its beauty had nothing to do with its history, or my own genetic attachment to it, or the work it made for me—which I enjoyed, since work, like solitude, gave me pleasure. It was not nostalgia (a certain rosy lie of fiction masquerading as history, which is its own kind of lie), nor the "happy valley" motif that invariably leads to blood feuds lasting for generations. It was simply that this was a place on Earth where the land appeared to be going about its work at almost the same rate as the resident humans were going about theirs; where the resident beasts, such as the owl, were right on the fence between wild and tame (if that fence was like most of my fences), morally wakeful without being fazed by consequences, like Eve and Adam with the fresh juice of the apple alive on their tongues, its flesh filling their cheeks, as they looked at each other with pleasure before that voice came out of the sky to tell them what they already knew as soon as they shared the thing.

I heard something fall, but it boinged rather than smashed, and was joined by a fluttering that told me the owl had found the dining room again. While I listened for the bird's wings to find their way into the open, I saw a dark square form break out and move downhill from behind the guesthouse, M. Braye's deserted cottage. I had never seen wild boar here before, though they were always said to inhabit the woods—*sangliers,* named after their habit of solitude (the Latin adjective *singularis*). This was a sow, or *laie,* as I knew because she was followed by six little ones, *marcassins,* all dew-covered and glowing as if with phosphorescence. The native color of the young boar should be fawn dappled with white, in stripes that would disappear with adolescence, but I could not see that because of the light they carried. The pigs cast black shadows that they dragged along with them to walk in, without which they would have seemed to float on moonstruck dew. When they reached the driveway, they turned to their left and trotted down the track with an assurance uncontaminated by stealth. I realized I had been holding my breath.

NINE

I had planned, after tea on that first day, to look over the second floor and get up to M. Braye's house. But as the afternoon elapsed, I'd been distracted by the plumber, and then, pleased at arriving and enjoying the flood of warm weather, I'd muttered, "The essence of civilization is denial," and taken the new imported hedge clippers out to the garden, hacked at the hedges awhile, and grabbed the opportunity to stroll around the property. I put on boots and walked down to the farthest fields above the de Longprés' house to see that the new apple trees (new, that is, twenty years ago) were surviving, and even preparing to bear fruit this year; to inspect the ruin of the cider press and determine whether it was more advanced (because a project for the future might be to roof it, then later to make something of it); to survey the ghost of my grandmother's walled kitchen garden, next to the old bakehouse, which was long gone, and the pumphouse, no longer in use; and finally to check the depth and population of the *douet*, the condition of the poplars alongside it, and the state of Mme. Vera's vegetable garden (as yet unplanted) next to the stream. From this last, I could look up at the house and see the attic windows blazing with the reflection of the late setting sun, and the second-story windows reproaching me with their closed shutters.

Beware nostalgia, something whispered, as if what I wanted here—disguised by the diaphanous garments of romance—was what had never been and never would be again. There was no way I could take this on and make it right, not if making it right meant making it what it might have been: that would be like trying to "restore" New Jersey. What was now a dwindling, run-down farm had once been a thriving settlement. The cider press, still worked in my grandparents' day, had been a thatched building larger than the house, its *grenier* filled in October with the farm's apples until it was time for the old horse, walking in circles, like Samson, around the now vanished circular trough, to grind them into juice that would ferment in the likewise vanished wooden tuns. The building was a ruin beyond repair, prob-

The cider press, 1928.

ably beyond any kind of rethinking: roofless and without openings for windows, it was still bigger than the house.

Recovering espaliered apple and pear trees towered against the cider press's naked brick and flint walls, whose warmth they still depended on. These were the fancy dessert trees my grandmother had planted, as Mme. Vera often bragged to me when I encountered her near the ruin, she perhaps climbing uphill with a basket of greens for her rabbits. Seeing the espaliered pear tree in flower, I realized that the other trees I had noticed blooming in the orchards might be pears in good health rather than apples uttering their last hurrah.

Near the cider press had stood a bakehouse where all the farm's bread was once made; now it was a dangerous pit masked by nettles and wild roses. The barn and all traces of it, meanwhile, had disappeared entirely, and the horse pond was a morass of impenetrable silt and marsh. It was here that the laundry of the Frieseke household had been scrubbed and beaten before being laid out on the grass to bleach. Within the walled kitchen garden that M. Braye had kept well into the sixties were two contiguous deep water tanks, made of brick and topped with floating scum, which I noticed had now been provided with some measure of protection from drowning large animals, in the form of a camouflage of rotting boards. I had never quite understood the tanks' purpose; they were part of the farm's old water supply, I knew, but beyond that I did not follow the plan. The stables where my grandmother had kept the cart she used to drive to market once a week in Pont l'Evêque, before they bought the Ford, and before Georges the White Russian refugee chauffeur, an ex-cossack, joined the household (Georges would later, in a fabled romance, marry Eugénie the cook, a native of Mesnil, and live with her after the war in Paris, where he found work at the

Soviet embassy)—those stables had been pulled down twenty years before, in hopeless ruin, the summer that a younger sister of mine had elected to be married in Mesnil. Following local custom, the whole town had been invited to the wedding.

The thatch on Mme. Vera's house was going faster than I had thought; its peak had already lost the iris that held the clay that in turn held the apex of the thatch. Most of the cement fence posts along the unkempt drive had been destroyed, and the old barbed wire strung between them dragged on the ground. Dead apple trees tipped over and loomed gaunt, and the pastures pullulated with thistles, nettles, dock, brambles, bracken, and other weeds deserving of no names. The farm I was in love with looked as if it were inhabited by Snopeses—who would be me if I became the proprietor of this place.

Thatching Mme. Vera's, 1968. Photo Mary Norris

"I am monarch of all I survey," I murmured to myself grimly, feeling more like Ozymandias than the shipwrecked Alexander Selkirk, better known under the alias Robinson Crusoe. Now thoroughly disheartened, I'd come back up to the house thinking I had better try to control *something*. From chests and closets I pulled rugs and curtains to make the entire first floor seem like a place that someone might live in on purpose. I hauled armloads of purple foxglove out of the woods—some with stems as tall as six feet—to give life and color to the interior, making a huge flourish of them on the table in the dining room, where they reached up like leaning caryatids to uphold the ceiling. Yellow broom was flowering in the woods, *Planta genista*, which the ancestors of England's Henry V had worn into battle on both sides of the Channel. They'd swept through this country with its blossoms stuck in their bonnets, leading to their family nickname, Plantagenet. Others—noncombatants—had, more significantly for the cause of civilization, made besoms of the same tough plant. I cut some of that also.

Next I walked around the first-floor rooms again, pointedly not looking for that wicker tray but still not coming upon it. Maybe the house was shabby, but shabby I had never minded; the illusion that the place was inhabited did me good.

One thing having led to another the day before, I had not got upstairs yet by the time I called Julia. I let her know there was nothing to collect on my flight insurance and waited, ready for her standard opening, "Is it beautiful?"

"There's still the flight back," Julia warned. She'd missed her cue. Instead of *Is it beautiful?* she was intent on the romance of air travel. She'd been talking with a friend who'd told her an airplane story she was eager to share. "It was a Chinese airline," she said, "but still . . ."

The narrative concerned a passenger plane that was flying over Szechuan when the pilot and copilot ran into the passenger compartment to check on some more-alarming-than-usual noise or smell. The door to their cabin flopped shut behind them and locked automatically to protect the cabin and controls from interference by hijackers—or, now, the pilot and copilot. As the stewardesses continued to bow along the aisles serving tea, the officers attacked the cockpit's door with fire axes while the plane . . .

"Jesus, you have to work your IQ down the bell curve until you get it way below the idiot level to ride an airplane. And how is everything there?" Julia asked with eager suspicion.

I began an enthusiastically favorable commentary on the weather and the solitude.

"That bad, eh?" Julia said.

"It's beautiful," I reminded her.

"Never mind beautiful," she replied. "Beautiful is always someone else's."

After that I gave in to jet lag, which the French call *le décalage horaire*—a *décalage* being, according to my dictionary, an unwedging or shifting of the zero. . . .

TEN

My night visitor meant that the next day, my second in Mesnil, I had to go to Pont l'Evêque, though I had not planned to leave the farm at all today. I did not, however, want the house to fill up with captive owls before the friends who were to rent it arrived. Animals keep strict routines: just as the wild sow and her young were liable to reappear at the same time in the same place at regular intervals (though not necessarily each morning), the owl might settle back into the dining room.

Smoke rose from Mme. Vera's chimney, but she herself was not visible when I looked outside, and I didn't go down to raise her. She knew I was here, and in due course she'd appear. Since we were such close neighbors, we were better off keeping out of each other's hair. After I cleaned up some of the fallen objects and had coffee, I drove my car down the driveway and into another amazing day of bright heat.

I kept meaning to stow an English-French dictionary in the car, but I generally forgot this until I was parked in front of M.

Mme. Vera's, 1995. Photo by author

Thouroude's hardware store. One of my primary functions in Normandy had long been to worry M. Thouroude, who, eager to help, invariably tried first to get me to explain to him what I planned to do, and then to persuade me not to.

As an American, I was weaned on self-service, for which the French term is, conveniently enough, *le self-service* (since it was not a French idea in the first place, no accommodation is made for it in the language of Racine). Likewise as an American, I am never fully prepared for the intimate role assumed by the small French merchant in any transaction. The first time Julia and I went together into a fabric store (in Lisieux), to buy curtain material for M. Braye's house, which we were working on—this was in the 1970s, after the Brayes died—we were met by two smiling, nicely dressed women who stood in front of a wall faced with closed drawers. Aside from the shop sign claiming they sold cloth, there was nothing whatever to see or point to—indeed nothing visible at all, apart from a large pair of shears on a counter, to prove that cloth of any kind was to be had here. When in France, Julia usually did her shopping by acting out what she wanted; she got on fine when it came to artichokes, eggs, or fish, but imitating the fabrics and patterns she had in mind was harder. And never, ever, must the customer touch the goods once the salesperson was tricked into showing them.

In France, the customer is never right. Even if we succeeded in buying something we wanted, which after all Madame had seemed prepared to sell, we had not won. When the bell on the shop door clanged on our departure, it was not with the cheerful peal that had first welcomed the victims, but rather with a mild reproving clang of dismay.

The first time I went into Lefebvre-Foinet, a French color-merchant's in Paris, intending to buy stretcher bars and canvas, I was asked, "What does Monsieur intend to paint?" It was as if, looking to buy a pair of socks, I must, before the clerk would risk her honor by showing me the garments, answer the question "And in what circumstances will Monsieur wear the socks?"

My French, never very good, became much worse in confrontation, but I managed to express bewilderment. The salesperson quickly understood that I was at a loss and explained with another question: "Is it landscape Monsieur wishes to execute, or seascape, or a portrait?" (*"Paysage, marine, ou figure?"*)

Not sure myself what I might paint, I certainly did not think it was any of *her* business. I might well stare at the naked canvas (*toile vierge*) until its virginity disturbed me more than anything I might do to violate it. The salesperson, with the exquisite, exasperated, kindly patience that comes only with generations of training, pulled out a card on which were printed all the dimensions available in stretched canvas, divided into three categories. The *paysage* selection comprised one kind of oblong; the *marine* another, more horizontal; the *figure* yet a third, more square.

I pointed to a vertical dimension from the *figure* category and a horizontal from the *paysage*. "Suppose I want to make a canvas this by this?"

"*Ah non, Monsieur,*" she told me. "*Ça ne se fait pas. C'est une fausse mesure.*" ("That is not done. That dimension is false, untrue, erroneous, wrong, spurious, base, counterfeit, forged, fictitious, sham, insincere, treacherous, deceitful, or equivocal.") She had me where she wanted me.

She glanced about her, signaling the *patron* by means of rapid eye movements. He came forward, smiling like a man with a blackjack in his pocket. I purchased some *figure* canvases and painted landscape on them.

Our American backgrounds made us clumsy in the French economy. We tiptoed around all the time, thus accidentally proving we had been *mal élevés* (ill brought up). The essence of an orderly society demands that each member know his or her place; otherwise, what can be the value of specialization? Therefore glass for the window is sold not at the *quincaillerie*, where fence posts may be had, but at the *droguerie*, where only a fool would seek to buy aspirin; it must then be handed over to a *vitrier* to be installed. Carpentry, for its part, should be done by a *menuisier* or a *charpentier* (depending on the grade of work required), never by the owner of the home.

Now, at M. Thouroude's *quincaillerie* in Pont l'Evêque, I realized that once again I did not have my dictionary with me and did not know what to call what I wanted; and remembered, too, that M. Thouroude had been watching for me since last summer, when I had let it slip within his hearing that rather than spending four hundred dollars on a ladder so as to replace some lost slates on the *auvent*, I proposed to make one myself using tree branches from the woods, relying only on the assistance of my equally misguided son Christopher (my eldest), who had come with me. M. Thouroude had begged me to be prudent, writing down the names and addresses of two roofers he recommended and assuring me that this was a matter for a professional. If I was not prepared at once to invest in repairs to the slate facing, well, all right: I could tell the roofer that my intention was to have the slates replaced someday. The roofer would merely drape the house in plastic until Monsieur was ready. Only over his own protest did M. Thouroude consent to sell me tar paper, roofing nails, and no ladder.

Steeling myself, I entered the *quincaillerie*. M. Thouroude, a tall, lean man in overalls, exactly the same age he had always been, came over to greet me—With a sad grin of sympathetic condolence? I wondered, or was I being overly sensitive?— "*Monsieur? Vous désirez?*"

I looked around the shop but saw nothing to point to among the firebacks, drill sets, spades, and spools of chain. Forced to fall back on narrative, I explained the problem of the owl. M. Thouroude listened with care and suggested that I close my windows before retiring. After I explained further, he wondered aloud if I planned to put up a fence around my house in order to keep the owls from entering.

No, I replied; the problem was the chimney. "Ah, well," M. Thouroude said, "there are persons who specialize in such things as chimneys. Do not take matters into your own hands,

Monsieur, I beg you. What you want is a *couvreur* [roofer] who will install a grille of the correct size at the top of your chimney. I can recommend two roofers. Talk to them both, then choose one."

No, I would do it myself, I said. I began to describe what I had in mind. The line of waiting customers grew and carefully appeared not to be listening. "But you would need to get up to the top of the chimney," M. Thouroude protested suspiciously. "You might fall." I did not flatter myself that he recalled my proposal to make my own ladder; nor, equally, could I flatter myself that he did not remember it.

When he at last understood that I was not to be dissuaded, M. Thouroude led me to the shed across the courtyard next to his shop, as I explained that I did not intend to risk my life in dealing with my owl problem. Spotting a tall roll of chicken wire resting among metal fence posts, scythes, posthole diggers, barbed wire, sacks of cement, ladders, stakes, and handles, I told him to cut me five meters. M. Thouroude insisted that for my own good, he must know how I intended to proceed.

"I'm going to roll it and stuff it up the chimney," I told him.

M. Thouroude shook his head and snipped dolefully: He would rather sell me nothing at all than participate in such a grave miscarriage of hardware. "The owls will continue to descend your chimney," he threatened. "And now, finding this wire for a foundation, they will build their nests on it and thus your chimney will fill with twigs and feathers and you will set fire to your house."

He wrote, with pencil on a paper bag, the names and addresses and phone numbers of two roofers whom he suggested I consult instead of going ahead with my rash strategy. He told me exactly how to find them, and the advantages and disadvantages of each. The line of customers waited, ostentatiously not taking notes, while M. Thouroude, advising, coiled my wire, tied it with twine, and wrapped it in heavy brown paper. He accepted my money and wrote out a receipt. For seven dollars I had obtained thirty minutes' worth of undivided attention from an expert.

ELEVEN

On my way back to the farm, I was delayed by cattle in the drive. The farmer who rented the fields raised beef, which was more and more the usual practice in these parts, replacing dairy farming. Milk products were subsidized, but dairy was labor-intensive, and the labor itself unremitting. Until five years earlier, Mme. Vera had milked her own twenty-some cows twice a day, by hand. My son Christopher (then fourteen) helped her the summer he stopped drinking milk. That same summer he learned that it was possible to eat twelve croissants at a sitting. He also learned everything about artificial insemination, as well as the other method applauded by the Pope of Rome, and about births and stillbirths and the thousand intimate ways cows and their excrement can intermingle.

What faced me in the drive—it was toward noon, still hot and dry, when I returned from my errand—was a bull, a couple of males too old for veal and too young for stud, and a passel of heifers, cows, and calves, the youngest of whom were totteringly new.

We had never found a way to keep the fences intact. Perhaps, as one friend, ecologically minded as only an urban visitor could be, had once suggested, they were contrary to the spirit of the place. The ones we built along the driveway immediately succumbed to mysterious maladies. According to the rental contract, it was the tenant's responsibility to maintain the fences. "*Ces gens là, il faut les prendre par le coeur*" ("These people, you have to grab them by the heart"), my mother once said, quoting a friend of hers from an older generation on how to get something done in the country. In my impetuous American way, I told my mother that maybe her friend was reaching too high.

The formal terms of our relationship—that is, of the relationship between Mme. Tonnelier, renter, and my mother, hereditary proprietor—were still maintained under the language of the relevant articles of the *Code Civil* of 1804, a replacement for the forelock-tugging, *droit-du-seigneur* approach of the old Norman usages as altered by the dictates of the newly created centralized state. Twice yearly, on the feast of Saint Michael (September 29) and on Christmas Day, in equal installments, rent was due to the tune of 180 kilograms of farmer's butter and 260 kilograms of second-rate beef (*viande de boeuf en deuxième qualité*), net weight. Fortunately for us, current practice was to render this *fermage* in its cash equivalent.

I herded the second-rate beasts out of the way with the car's horn. The fields along the driveway were busy with magpies, and I both saw and heard the pair of hawks hunting above as I drove up toward the house. Mme. Vera was busy in the fenced yard in front of her house, a hundred feet from mine, washing the slab of cement that was part of her courtyard with a stiff broom and water from a hose, under a broad sky of brilliant blue across which fat clouds rushed, high up and in opposite directions to

Mme. Vera's courtyard, 1988. Photo Walter Chapin

each other, making fast shadows swirl across the green hillside, as if the world were being stirred with a long-handled spoon.

Mme. Vera was surrounded by dogs, ducks, and chickens, as well as a slinking outrider of feral cats. I drove the car down to the broad area next to the thatched garage attached to her house, originally built for the Friesekes' Ford and later considered by my parents as a suitable place to store the Citroën during the winter. The spirit of the place preferred otherwise, however, so they arranged for active storage with the Citroën *garagiste* in Pont l'Evêque, from whom I had hidden the day

Mme. Vera's courtyard, 1988. Photo Walter Chapin

before. The addition at the far end of her cottage had been built on as my grandfather's studio, though he often painted in the house. That space, like the garage and much of the remainder of Mme. Vera's quarters, now served as a general storage area and chicken run.

Mme. Vera threw her arms around me and we began to exchange kisses. A woman of eighty who had lived a hard life for many years, she had blossomed with old age and widowhood. Today she was wearing a pretty dress printed with pink flowers. I had noticed some of her laundry hanging on the metal clothesline next to my house when I arrived; by the time I looked out in the morning, it had migrated to her own line, further down the hill. Mme. Vera was now bent almost as badly as her husband had been in his time, and her husband's father, M. Braye; but she seemed healthy. Her hands were big and square and twisted, and she still exuded a pleasant smell of cider mixed with milk just on the edge of turning sour.

I hunkered down (mentally) and prepared to converse. In talking with Mme. Vera, the language was not the problem, since she was a fellow foreigner and spoke French more clearly than I had a right to expect (she was also, it was said, fluent in Russian, Polish, and German); rather, it was the content. Mme. Vera was permanently inspired by disaster, and filled with rumor. She had an unyielding memory for catastrophe but with the cruel advance of age had gradually lost her sense of time as a discipline by which to organize phenomena, so that all past events now existed in her conversation, unless this was a function of my own confusion, as if they had happened only the day before yesterday. She and I were tied together by links of mutual gratitude and wariness extending many years into the past. Because I was contemplating becoming of the owning, while she would remain of the renting, class, I could not avoid taking in many of her observations with a guilty sense that it was up to me to set matters right. We swapped good wishes and family information before she started telling me her news, acting it out as she narrated it.

Ah, the things that had happened! There had been terrible storms. Two cows had been struck by lightning and had to be buried—as everyone knew, a cow struck by lightning could not be eaten. The meat perished instantly! The ground had been so wet that nothing could be planted. All the seeds had rotted. Everything had died in the ground. It was a disaster. Because of the drought, everything had withered and died. The cows that lived had got infections and aborted. Bombs had fallen back in the woods, and a piece of the house had been knocked off. There were almost no rabbits. Dead, all dead. Barely a chicken was left. A tourist had fired a rifle at her goats. Unspeakable! Everything was so expensive. How could a person eat? There was no sugar anywhere. Prices for beasts had gone down, and a man had died before the ambulance could reach him. Life was hard. The linden trees had gone, with one falling limb almost killing a child.

I listened sympathetically to these complaints, but without the alarmed surprise I had felt on first hearing them, since many of them dated from before 1968 (including the one about the cows struck by lightning, now the stuff of fable) or, in the case of the bombs in the woods, from much earlier still. But life remained hard.

"It is so sad, cher Monsieur, the way the château"—the *house* I was sleeping in could be called a château only by the most elastic indulgence, but in this instance the honorific was meant as both compliment and accusation, since it accentuated my being on the "owning" side of the fence and Mme. Vera's being on the "renting" (never mind that we were both aware that the spirit of the place was inimical to fencing)—"the way the château is closed all the time," Mme. Vera said, looking mournful and acting out the part of the shuttered house. "And the linden trees—I remember well how dear Monsieur Frieseke would stroll under those trees in the evenings after dinner"—here she made herself look stout and male, placing her hands behind her back, seeming to be smoking a cigarette, and strutting slowly—"and how I caught him in my own arms when he died." She did a pantomime of that event, playing both parts: my grandfather, having hurried back from the café in Mesnil with news of the impending war, succumbing to a stroke or a heart attack; and herself, then a brawny girl, catching him as he fell. She had often shown me the spot where it had happened, which corresponded with the place where my parents had first met each other, under my bedroom window; and I recalled my grandmother's recounting how she herself had baptized her husband then, as he had asked her to do, theirs having been, up till that moment, a marriage between a vehement Catholic Democrat and an ambivalent Protestant Republican. I think, however, that he died still true to the Republican party.

Afterward, with the war closing over Europe, my grandmother had offered to find passage for them both and to bring Vera with her to the States, but Vera, no longer able to take her dowry back to Poland, instead invested in a local love. She and M. Tonnelier, remaining on the property during the German occupation, had interceded as best they could on behalf of what my grandmother had left behind, and farmed out her possessions for safekeeping; one vivid tale had M. Tonnelier climbing into the woods carrying a large nude of Frieseke's. It always seemed a grotesque ingratitude to complain about the fences: it was only on account of the Tonneliers that we had anything left at all.

The mimed death of my blood relation was a standard part of Mme. Vera's repertory, reminding me of the queasy feeling that had come over me when, at the age of twelve or so, I first watched the movie *The Fighting 69th*, in which my other grandfather, my father's father, the poet Joyce Kilmer, played by Jeffrey Lynn, is shot, and mourned over by Pat O'Brien in the role of Fighting Father Duffy. He was buried (not Jeffrey Lynn, but Joyce Kilmer) in the American military cemetery in Fère-en-Tardenois. Leaving a wife and children in New Jersey, he had signed up and come to France in 1918 on a troop ship to serve with the Fighting 69th, and been killed in action later that year. Three of my four grandparents, therefore, were buried in France.

While Mme. Vera talked and my mind wandered, the courtyard in front of her house seethed with her animals: the chickens and ducks, and the cats, and an old dog so lame it rolled more than it could be said to walk. Her rabbits chewed in their hutches behind a propped-up wooden picnic table decorated with plastic geraniums and dahlias. A sudden barrage of rifle fire from downhill that startled me back into war for a minute proved to be nothing more than the young kids dancing on the rusty corrugated iron roof that covered part of the cider press: Mme. Vera's goats were taking the sun there, and the little ones were impatient with the elders' nap.

I had known the pair of linden trees that Mme. Vera had referred to, under which she claimed Frieseke had once strolled after dinner. They used to stand at the end of the house closest to her, casting permanent shade across it and filling, in June, with sweet flowers and bees, scenting the humming rooms beneath them with honey, mildew, and vanilla. The lindens had succumbed one after the other about ten years previously, but not before Mme. Vera had advised me one summer to slip an armload of their blooms secretly into Julia's mother's bath, should she give me any trouble. Linden flowers had a pacifying effect, Mme. Vera assured me.

Julia's mother had joined us that first summer. She was always ready to participate in a good time, and France had long been one of her favored stamping grounds. In the bloom of youth, sent off to be "finished" by way of a European tour, after the chaperon gave up and died during the ocean voyage, she had spent her entire travel allowance immediately upon her arrival in Paris, buying herself handmade underwear. When Julia and I were preparing to make our first trip to Normandy, she offered us a few travel tips. Christopher was just two years old then, and we were availing ourselves of the cheapest possible travel, a propeller-driven Icelandic Airways flight via Reykjavík to Luxembourg, where we were to find a train to Paris, change stations, and locate another train. Our country, having just lost Martin Luther King and Bobby Kennedy, was in upheaval, and heading into the political turmoil of a hard campaign summer. During that spring of 1968, our student friends in Cambridge had reminded us excitedly that the revolution then in progress in the States was full-blown in Paris, complete with posters and flying cobblestones and riot police. The students in France's cities were trying to establish common cause with indifferent working people whom they categorized as *ouvriers* and *paysans.* Julia and I could be part of all that, our friends said enviously.

As we left loaded with our ignorance and baggage, Julia's mother's parting advice was, "Naturally, you cannot afford even a cup of tea at the Paris Ritz, but if you put on your best clothes (those *aren't* your best clothes, are they?), you can go in and use the ladies' room there, Julia, while Nick holds the baby in the lobby or, better, in the street outside. Just the ladies' room will give you the whole idea and is well worth a detour. You can tell Nick all about it afterward."

So Julia's mother still loved a good time, and came to swell the house party. Julia's father, a more sedate and cautious individual who liked his comfort, used the flimsy excuse of having to remain available to patients needing surgery to justify staying home in Illinois.

What Julia's mother found in Mesnil was eleven people in a house with an undependable roof, no running water, and no electricity, and so she took the precaution of spending her nights in a hotel nearby. Joining us during the day, she used to look around her as she sat in the salon playing solitaire, always eager to participate in the next event, whether a baptism or a marketing expedition or a *goûter* (high tea) with one of the ancient ladies in the neighborhood. One of us would come tracking through the room with materials intended to shore up some act of temporary rehabilitation, and she would exclaim, "Good night!" before quoting the mantra of her own midwestern mother (who had lived in brick in Beardstown, Illinois): "A house is greedy."

Writing home to a friend at the end of one such day, Julia's mother preserved (though not, she thought, for publication) some of the flavor of her perception of that summer of '68.

August 19th, night

Such a glorious day. This morning I met Frances in the Pont l'Evêque marché. En verité she did this for me because you can buy most everything anyway and not have such big crowds. Anyhoo—I arrived at the marché hunting for her and I felt I was at the local IGA. First I met Mme. Després, then Mlle. Gabry and Mme. Rohe, and Mme. Lafontaine and Mlle. Margot Lafontaine, then finally Frances. It was such a glorious day we decided on a picnic so we bought cheese and lettuce and and and—Put in car. Then we bought paté *and* jambon *and* cornichons *and ? and put in car. Then we bought bread and cakes etc. and put in car and took it all home, filled our* paniers *and off for a picnic on a hill. It was lovely and we loved it.*

Then because it was such a clear day six of us went to Honfleur. This included a charming fourteen-year-old English boy who is visiting someone near and arrived as we were leaving.

Went first to little church high on Côte de Grace with the panorama where because of clear day we felt Le Havre to be only a spit away. Then down into town to see the bell tower and English church and the Boudins in the musée. *Loved it and thought of you. Julia and Nick think it is a little Rockportish but I am less jaded and loved it. All around the harbor then and back for dinner—tongue with an interesting sauce of shallots, vinegar, capers, ?, potatoes and carrots from garden, and string-bean salad. This done by J. and N. who stayed home. Nick is working soooo madly to finish bookshelves so they can unbury the collection in cupboards and with friends. (Tell you right now there are not ever going to be enough bookcases.)*

These women sure talk a convincing line of doom, I told myself, exchanging more kisses with Mme. Vera before pulling myself away from something she was saying about a flood. Noah's, maybe—but still, worth a worry.

TWELVE

I brought my roll of wire into the dining room and propped it next to the fireplace, poured oil and vinegar over the remains of last night's supper, pulled out a book of birds, and looked for my owl. Among the nocturnal raptors listed, I figured it might be either the *petit duc* (this was, after all, supposed to be a château) or the *effraie* (a barn or screech owl), which favored ruins. The latter was said to pluck its prey messily, to favor a regular eating place, and to keep a larder, its diet consisting in: birds, 1 percent; mammals (bats, mice, field mice, voles, shrews), 95 percent; frogs and toads, 2 percent; and insects, 1 percent. Any and all of these culinary delights could be living somewhere in the building where I was eating my own solitary lunch. There was always a supply of bats in the attic, and I vividly recalled a large toad's having set up shop one year in the hole that accommodated the sluggish drainpipe from the downstairs kitchen sink, through which water was carried out into the fields.

Another failing of mine that Julia frequently pointed out was

that I didn't always put my marbles away before I started playing with my blocks and train set. Looking around now, I realized
I was already halfway into about seven projects of revision and
rearrangement and unpacking and exploring, none of which I
could remember starting but the sum of which already threatened to swamp this room. The night before, I'd reached for a fork
to eat my supper with and had to chase around the room until I
found where the O'Banyons had preferred to keep the tableware;
then and there I'd started putting it back where I wanted it by
laying it out first on the table. Julia's cloths were spread across
the couch; I'd had to pull out a number of books to settle on the
best choice to describe my owl—and so on. It was true that even
in a state of solitude I tended to proliferate. *Like a sea urchin,*
Julia said, *that just keeps shooting seeds into the ocean. No wonder you want a big house; you're going to fill it up, too, wherever
it isn't already filled with everyone else's stuff. The ocean's only so
big, as we're finding out, you know, these days.*

I needed to work if I wanted to move if I wanted to live,
though, which always seemed to include an aspect of expansion.
But even so, while drinking my coffee I made a careful and clear-
eyed analysis of past performance and concluded that in spite of
my appearing to agree with Julia's opinion, if I did not fabricate
my blockade in the chimney at once, I would end up having to
dodge the roll of wire for days, or losing it under something, or
finding another use for it.

I knew enough about chimneys to take my clothes off first in
order to save having to wash them after. I was not going to be
here long; if I washed clothes, I would have to try the temperamental washing machine, and anything I washed I would then be
obliged to dry by grace of the equally temperamental weather.
My task was simple and easily done. After five minutes' work

inside the chimney, I thought I might try the new shower, which I had never used since it had been completed only the year before, on the very morning I was leaving. That would also get me upstairs for the first time.

I climbed the grand if decaying staircase past the jam closet. My habit, like that of my forebears, was to hold my breath and speed up when passing the jam closet, like a child skirting a graveyard. It took up the space between me and the salon on the right side as I climbed to the second floor. I imagined the staircase to be an addition of the late sixteenth century, since prior to that no one would have wanted to expend precious interior space on stairs: in Norman country houses, the expected route from first to second floors was via an outside staircase on one end of the building. What had originally been a simple square room in the center of each of the first three floors had thus later been disrupted by these interloping staircases, and by the various uses (such as the jam closet and the bathroom over it) to which the excess space around the stairs had been put. Because the ceilings of the first floor were so low, the staircase crossed the width of the house in one straight run and led through double doors into the corridor upstairs along the west side, onto which all the rooms on that floor opened. I turned south (or left) along the hallway I had lined with bookshelves, hunting for a towel. The architect Mesnier, when he reenvisioned the house in the early nineteenth century, had intended it to be entered, for formal purposes, through a double door at the foot of the stairs, which we never opened. Through this door Mesnier had been able to welcome, directly from the garden, guests who had been obliged to walk around the outside of the house, under the library windows. The front doors, when thrown open to the garden, immediately prohibited lateral inward motion, blocking as they did the jam closet on one side and, on the other, the dining room (which in those days was the kitchen.)

When you turned left at the top of the stairs, the first room you came to was the billiard room. This room, the second in from the south end, connecting to what became my mother's bedroom by a walk-through closet, was paneled in oak that had survived the refugees. Above its fireplace, faced in green marble, was the only date I ever found in the house, inlaid in wood between couchant billiard cues over the mirror: 1836, following the joined family names, Mesnier-Bréard, of the couple responsible for a number of the building's improvements. It was the Mesnier-Bréards who had reoriented the house to face east and tricked the facade into looking like stone; they who had added paneling to many rooms, and clothed the walls of dining room, staircase, and upstairs corridor in plaster meant to mimic (once again) their beloved, dismal stone; they who had painted the woodwork around the doors to resemble marble, and certain of the marble fixtures to resemble wood. It was they who had designed the garden's terraces.

If, like me, you enjoy digging up the root meanings of words (it is another, efficient way to ensure that no flat surface will be without its heap of reference materials), you may be interested to learn that a *mesnier* was originally a man "attached" to a house, a domestic or officer of some kind, perhaps corresponding to an English steward (which itself yields the name Stewart). *Mesnier* has the same root as *Mesnil*. This part of Normandy is known as the Pays d'Auge because an *auge* is a trough or a valley, in this case primarily that of the River Touques. The word *auge* "evokes humidity," according to my book on the meanings of Norman place names, which now lay open on the dining table downstairs. (A table with room for ten diners could accommodate many works-in-progress, so long as I enjoyed my solitary free run of this place.) Our corner of the Pays d'Auge is filled with towns that include *mesnil* in their names. Usually denoting a location established as the equivalent of a manor prior to the time of Charlemagne, the word appears on the map in a number of variants—*magny, mangny, masnil, many, masny, menus*—all of which suggest our *mansion* (French *maison*) and mean, roughly, "domain." *Le Mesnil Mauger* thus means "Mauger's domain." That the nearest settlement to me had been named more than a thousand years before came as no surprise, given that a Roman road passed through Mesnil. What was more, the Roman roads themselves followed existing tracks carved into the land either by game or by the indigenous Gallic tribe whose name their Roman conquerors recorded as Lexovii (after whom Lexovium, or Lieuvin, now Lisieux, where they had a fortified encampment, took *its* name).

The Romans left a legacy of place names, and the Vikings (or Normans) interposed others. You can map the territorial successes of the Viking raiders in the Norman region (as well as their ferocity), after their invasions of the ninth and tenth centuries, by the incidence of the Nordic word *bec*, meaning "stream." The stream that cut between our hill and Mont Ange (Mount Angel) opposite, from which peak the mule sang in the early morning— I had heard it this very day—was sometimes known as the Virebec, or Vitrebec. The composer Charles Gounod once addressed a poem to it that my neighbor Mme. de Longpré had often promised to show me. Gounod had also selected the organ that continued to pontificate on special occasions in Notre Dame du Mesnil, under the influence of that same neighbor.

I'd heard threats of rain from Mme. Vera, and the clouds were active, but the day outside the billiard room's shutters, when I opened them for light to find a towel by, was still hot and dry.

My grandparents had used the billiard room as their bedroom. Fred enjoyed the game, which he played with fellow members of the American Artist Club in Paris, but he kept no table in Normandy. Julia and I had expected our children to sleep in this room when they were young, since we occupied the adjacent chamber and so could get to them easily through the passage closet during the night. Because of its scabbed oak paneling, however, they found the room gloomy, despite its view of the garden's pond and topiary yew tree. (The latter was recovering even more triumphantly than my grandmother's espaliered fruit trees; there was no sign now of its former basket shape.) I looked down at what had been hawthorn and box hedges, now outrageously overgrown into sagging walls of green. The hawthorn was in bloom.

Tea in the garden, 1928. (Left to right, Agnes Walsh O'Bryan, Mrs. Frieseke, Frances, Mr. Frieseke.) Photo Grattan O'Bryan

In spite of the fact that the door opening onto the corridor had a glass panel that allowed light to enter from that side as well, our daughter Maizie always claimed that the only reason the room did not fill up with witches at night was that witches were afraid of spiders. Although it was too late to improve the room's ambience for the children, I had recently installed a mural in segments occupying panels all around the room; taking advantage of the windows and mirrors, it adapted the circular pond in the garden, so that when you stood in the center of the room, you felt you were also in the midst of the pond, which had somehow lifted itself out of the garden and into the house. Should the house become mine, it was my seditious intent sacrilegiously to violate this somber chamber by painting the wood panels white.

The billiard room's main purpose now was to hold the linen closet. I pulled out a towel for my delayed shower and noticed that the volume of sheets and towels seemed much diminished this year. I am not good at sheets, but I do have a memory for bulk, and the bulk of cloth was considerably less. If linens were missing, as well as the wicker tray . . . how easily might the other furnishings of this house I thought to take over wander out into the countryside?

Now that I had opened the room's windows to the unusual hot breeze and sunlight, I was obliged to sweep up the hordes of dead flies and bees that had collected at the end of the corridor next to my mother's bedroom, under the southwest window, where they invariably gathered when the house was closed. Then I went for my reward.

The second-floor bathroom occupied the same centrally located corner as the jam closet and entrance hall beneath it. It was narrow and L-shaped, and when you stood in the corridor at the top of the grand stairway, facing down, with the bathroom door on your left (once painted a hideous fake faux-oak and more recently desecrated by me with a *couche* of plain "French" gray semi-gloss house paint), you could look across the stairwell at a wall into which were set two little windows that provided an unobstructed view of the bathroom's activities—unless, that is, the occupant had thought to draw the curtains inside. The intention behind this arrangement was to allow daylight from the bathroom's garden window to reach the stairwell, but unwitting or unwarned visitors sometimes found things getting rather informal when they or someone in the family who wished to shower crossed the gauntlet of those two windows.

This bathroom could also be entered from the bedroom adjacent to it on the side that was not a stairwell, by means of a low doorway into which a step had been inserted. This could give the early riser a rude awakening if it didn't knock him out, but it picked up one of the architectural themes of the floor below. With the advent of the new shower, the third entrance that the bathroom once enjoyed—via the passage closet into the billiard room—had been suppressed.

I walked in to take my maiden joy of the shower and learned that the bathroom could now also be entered through the floor.

I stood agape. The plumber's *gars* the day before had tactfully refrained from mentioning that the floor of the *salle d'eau* had essentially rotted out. Or had he assumed I knew and, being an American, simply accepted the fact that I could stare down through openings between the tiles into the darkness of the jam closet below? The toilet, repaired the previous year by the same large men who had installed the shower in this little room, was evidently still leaking. It was impossible to guess how much support, if any, might remain under the tiles. I tiptoed out of the room, distributing my weight as broadly as I could.

If bathing was my primary concern, I had an alternative to the new shower: the six-foot tub in the first floor *salle d'eau*, off the salon and connecting to the guest bedroom. This bathroom, because it was at the far end of the house from the furnace room, had been provided with its own hot-water heater, a geyser that ran on propane tanks, which I would have to drag out of the downstairs kitchen and hook up myself outside. Once the geyser's pilot was lighted, the force of the cold water running through the thermostat was supposed to cause a plume of fire to heat the flow to tub or basin. As with my parents' Citroën *familiale*, I hated the heater as much as I distrusted it. It was fine when it worked, but the flame liked to blow itself out just as its victim attained the point of no return, and I worried that I was endangering my soul whenever I tried to light the pilot.

With a spirit that M. Thouroude would have recognized I determined to make the upstairs bathroom safe enough to let me damn well take my shower. Was I not the potential master of this house, and monarch of all I surveyed? I was certainly dressed for it, if I'd learned nothing else from the story of the emperor's new suit. I put on a pair of pants and went to have a look in the *cave* for some planks with which to rig a temporary emergency floor.

The *cave* was the ground-floor storeroom where we tried to keep tools and lumber. The room next to it, under the first-floor bathroom, was used to house firewood, though there were signs that the spirit of the place had also moved Mme. Vera's goats to shelter here during the winter. To reach the *cave* I first had to go outdoors. Along the west side of the house, next to the driveway, on the level that, because it was below the first one acknowledged to be habitable, was called the *sous-sol*, were five rooms. Only two of these, the downstairs kitchen and the laundry room at the center, connected either to each other or to the *rez-de-*

chaussée—which I, being American, insisted on calling the first floor, while what I called the second floor was what the Mesnier-Bréards would have termed the first.

The *cave*, directly below the salon, could be entered only from the driveway, though it could be seen into from the laundry room through a small window called a *meurtrière*, through which an early defender of the house could have shot arrows at any besieger misguided enough to break in via the *cave*. This was the only one of the auxiliary rooms that had a functioning lock, the single existing antique key to which hung from a supporting post in the kitchen—unless, of course, it had been mislaid.

I tell you, it's too much, I heard Julia's voice whispering. But the *cave*'s key was in its place. *You see? Don't be such a pessimist,* I answered. The doves groaned above me as I stood barefoot in the driveway and opened the *cave* door to the loud sound of rushing water. A freshet poured through a big hole in a joint of one of the lead pipes that carried cold water along the ceiling, in the direction of the downstairs bathroom. The leak was so exuberant that I would have noticed it the day before had I not been bemused by jet lag and my pleasure at being here—*and, maybe, by the ridiculous size of the house,* Julia whispered. Gallons a minute were gushing out, soaking the walls and floor and, worse, the supporting (?) beams and rafters. Tracing the pipes into the wood room and back again through the laundry and the kitchen, I found numerous other small leaks, some in joints and others in the pipes themselves. The worst of these played musically onto the stored lumber, as it must have done for most of the previous summer—the O'Banyons' summer, I realized I was calling it. I now understood the feeling of terminal damp I had encountered on first entering the house the day before, which no amount of hot air from the outside over the past two days had been able to alleviate. The place was a springhouse on at least two floors, one right above, and the other just below, the salon.

Tell me again how we're going to manage this? Julia's voice worried while I unfolded a plastic tarp and, using clothespins and wire, rigged a sluice to channel the main flow out of the *cave* and into the driveway before I carried boards upstairs to make a catwalk across the tiles. My plan was to distribute my weight evenly between any joists that might still exist, though a furtive glance at the ceiling of the jam closet suggested that such working joists were in the minority. What I could see of the jam closet's packed contents comprised mainly fallen mud and rotted wood, with a spray of mushrooms—blind, inedible, albino versions of the *Hypholoma capnoides,* my mushroom book seemed to confirm—growing from the wall and ceiling below the toilet.

I took my shower.

There, I told Julia, shining with cleanliness. *A child could do it. Nothing to it. See? I've been here only two days, and I've already managed to wash.*

I turned off the water and the electricity and called Mme. Le Planquay.

THIRTEEN

The clatter of the doorbell in the downstairs kitchen that evening announced company: Thérèse Chevalier. She'd seen my light the night before from her house across the hill from Mme. Vera's, and since she was off to her apartment in Paris the next morning, she had come up to say hello.

Black clouds had frisked across the sun and stayed there late in the afternoon and, after deliberating and waning, had spread to deliver a steady drizzle. Thérèse wore boots and a yellow slicker and carried an umbrella, having walked across the fields between her house and mine.

Thérèse was of the generation poised between mine and my parents', just as her own parents fell squarely between my parents and grandparents. She had spent much of her childhood in Mesnil. She and her mother (her father was then at sea) had been among those who walked from Paris into the countryside under a rain of German bullets as the French capitulated to the Germans in June of 1940. They were in Caen when it was bombed by the allies in June of 1944, and they walked from the flaming ruins of that city to Mesnil while the D-day invasion was in progress. On her mother's side, Thérèse was a member of the extensive Lafontaine family, which descended on Mesnil every August from its varied winter quarters elsewhere in France and North Africa, historically making up half the town's summer population. She was unmarried, funny, charming, and intelligent; a former teacher of history at a French university, she spoke perfect English. For several years she had been what she called retired, but I had never known anyone more in love with her profession. She had turned history into her hobby now that she was no longer teaching—but she hadn't really stopped teaching, either, since she was always on the lookout for a new student. Thérèse, like the ancient mariner, loved nothing better than to hold you with her glittering eye and reveal to you her most recent cache of research. I knew what was coming.

Thérèse left her wet things in the downstairs kitchen and followed me upstairs for a cup of tea next to the fire. We sometimes went years without seeing each other, though we had the familiarity common to siblings widely separated by age. She looked around approvingly at my informal arrangements in the dining room, particularly the books that were piling up on every available surface.

"Good to see you settling in," Thérèse said. She was not one of those visitors who muttered, shook their heads, and said something along the lines of *O, what a noble house is here o'erthrown*, though she had known it when my grandparents lived here, at which time it had indeed been more finished, furnished, and coherent. For one thing, it had not yet been vandalized for heat then: the refugees had burned bookshelves, paneling, and closet doors, as well as furniture. But nonetheless, even in my grand-

The salon with Mrs. Frieseke, 1937. Photo Claude Giraud

parents' day, the effect had been threadbare and eclectic (or as
Saint-Gaudens more tactfully put it, "completely colorful"). My
grandfather, always a domestic painter, had preferred to work in
the house, and many of the paintings he did after 1920 showed

furnishings we could still point to. My grandmother would rush about the house second-guessing and sweeping surfaces before him as he roamed in search of a subject or vantage point; she hoped to prevent him from recording as still-life what to her eyes (and, she believed, to anyone else's) looked like clutter that would shame her as a housekeeper when the resulting paintings were hung at the Salon of the Société Nationale des Beaux Arts in Paris, or at Macbeth's gallery in New York.

"But the gardens were something else," Thérèse said. "There was nothing neglected about your grandmother's gardens. Oh, the stories she would tell. Mae West, and Buffalo Bill, and bandits in New Mexico; and how she would dress everyone in costume for a birthday or a fête. She was so much fun. Such a shame your grandfather never learned French. I followed him in the field while he was painting, and he never said a word."

In fact, my grandfather knew French perfectly well, but as it was explained to me, he did not speak if he had nothing to say. My grandmother, in contrast, like Julia, was a gregarious, compelling, adept, and entertaining talker who was sometimes obliged on social occasions to make do for the two of them.

Thérèse and I sat on either side of the fireplace and listened to the rain splash against the slates and occasionally find its way down the chimney in drops large enough to hiss on the embers. We ran through recent family news as the tea steeped, covering the necessary groundwork while Thérèse clearly itched to include me in her present obsession—or obsessions (plural), it turned out.

The following day, she must rush off to Paris for her regular session with the life models whom the government made available to the citizens of Paris. She was drawing and painting seriously now. Then she must hurry back as soon as she could to

Normandy to continue gathering bits of research that would connect Mesnil and its environs to the larger picture.

She dropped three lumps of sugar into her tea and stirred—paused—and let the full joy of her project start to unfold.

"My idea is a history of Mesnil, starting in the Cretaceous period, when we were all underwater here where we are sitting, and the animals were laying down their chalk shells to make this hill. Then I'll move slowly forward to the present day, always with Mesnil as the focus—but I don't know, what do you think? Does it matter that there are only about thirty people at any given time in Mesnil who might be able to read it, or want to? But it could be great. Some interesting people have been here. Charles Gounod, of course, the composer who wrote the 'Ave Maria'; everyone knows he was an important character around here. You've probably heard a thousand times how he met the Count of Mesnil while walking on the beach in Trouville in 1846, and they became friends for life. Gounod had almost drowned—he was older; the count was just a kid at the time, twelve, at the beach with the priest who was also his tutor. So there's Gounod. But there were others, too.

"You know Guillaume Apollinaire, the poet? Right on the first day of the First World War, he was so near your house you could have thrown a rock and hit him." Thérèse seemed to be looking into the fireplace for a rock of the right size; one of the fossilized clamshells from the hill would be about right. "He'd been in Deauville with a friend and because of the mobilization they had to drive back to Paris to enlist, which they did via the road that goes through Pont l'Evêque and Lisieux. He had a flat tire near here, which he made famous in a poem he wrote in the shape of a little car—look, I'll show you—with a driver and two passengers."

She pulled a Xeroxed page out of her bag.

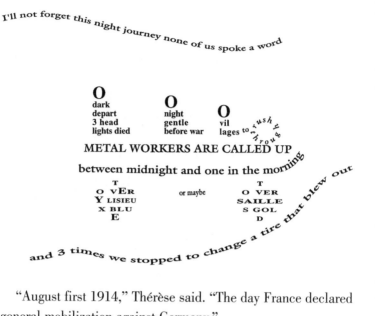

I'll not forget this night journey none of us spoke a word

O
dark
depart
3 head
lights died

O
night
gentle
before war

O
vil
lages to rush through

METAL WORKERS ARE CALLED UP

between midnight and one in the morning

T
O vER
Y LISIEU
X BLU
E

or maybe

T
O VER
SAILLE
S GOL
D

that blew out

and 3 times we stopped to change a tire

"August first 1914," Thérèse said. "The day France declared general mobilization against Germany."

If it was history she was after, I had something to toss in. I told her how my mother had also responded to the mobilization call as best she could, though she was a day late: she was born in Paris on August 2, 1914.

We talked of how the illustrated newspapers from the period just before that war read as if everyone believed that all the armaments and uniforms were being prepared for a parade of limited and specified duration and direction. Although many of the Americans residing in France left just before or during the onset of the war, the Friesekes had remained, in Paris and in Giverny, where the sounds of cannon fire had interrupted my grandfather's painting by making his models jump.

The Friesekes had no car then, and would not until the Ford and Georges the chauffeur. My grandfather did attempt some patriotic driving for the Red Cross ambulance service during the

The Friesekes with the Ford.

hostilities, but it wasn't long before everyone acknowledged that he endangered more than just the wounded whenever he got behind the wheel: always drawn by landscape, he tended to follow his eye. He was transferred to bedpan duty and rather quickly went back to painting.

The evening darkened outside, and the rain intensified. I had always wanted to ask Thérèse about some of her father's stories. During the first years of our visits, Alain Chevalier had been generous with his time, driving us here and there and telling us stories.

During the Second World War, after he came back from the sea, Alain had told us, when the house Thérèse and I now sat in was occupied by the Germans, he had kept a clandestine radio at his house in Mesnil, using, for an aerial, a metal clothesline. What did Thérèse remember of this?

Thérèse looked blank and slightly uncomfortable, as if the specifics of her father's tale had some negative impact on her view of the big picture. She dodged. There was so much war, she said, in the region's history. After the Romans, and following several centuries of something like peace (albeit a chaotic and dangerous one), Viking river boats of shallow draft, like the flatboats or *gabarres* used by local traders, had penetrated the land of the Pays d'Auge by way of the River Touques, which meandered northward through broad marshes and welcomed the raiders at its mouth, emptying into what English-speakers called the English Channel at what was now Deauville. In 1944 the German forces of occupation had manned a large gun emplacement in the same spot, overlooking what French maps used to refer to as Le Canal de France but now termed La Manche (the sleeve). That battery had been part of the defense of the Seine estuary, across from Le Havre.

"But your father?" I pressed her.

As far as what her father had done during the war . . . Thérèse could not recall anything about a secret radio in Mesnil.

"During the war," I continued, "at the time of the D-day invasion, when the bombing was widespread—I've heard that forty bombs fell just in this commune—the citizens of Mesnil, with their cows, according to your father, took refuge in a cave in the hill across the valley. . . ."

Thérèse looked more uncomfortable. Even seated next to the fireplace she was tall, and she was sweet, with her father's warmth and wit. But she was also as pious and as devoted to the truth as had been her mother before her. She said, "You know, my father . . . unfortunately, my father really enjoyed a good story."

FOURTEEN

But I've been in the cave," I protested. "Your father crammed a bunch of us into his 'Deux Chevaux' one afternoon twenty years ago, with Julia's mother next to him up front, and took us across the valley. We went up through woods and fields until we got to the mouth of a limestone cave hidden among nettles and brambles. When we went down into it, it seemed easily large enough for the population of the town. I remember galleries, and a ceiling supported by columns, and that limestone smell like my downstairs kitchen. We walked around in that cave. The children shouted for the echoes. I've been there. No doubt about it," I insisted.

Only reluctantly, and briefly, did Thérèse pull her mind out of the more interesting ancient past. "Maybe. That would be where they mined the stone for the church," Thérèse said. "A quarry. The first church in Mesnil—you can still see one arch of it—was built in the tenth or eleventh century, when William the Conqueror's family was covering the country with what historians call a 'white mask of churches.' Most of the present building dates from the thirteenth century, after the first church was torn down. Who knows why? The tower came later. Anyway, I suppose the quarry could have been a refuge for the townsfolk of Mesnil when Edward III of England swept through, looting and pillaging, on his way from the Cotentin to Crécy and Calais, which those Rodin Burghers turned over to him in 1347. Edward had to pass through Lisieux, not all that far from here. It's interesting that you should mention your mother's birthday, because Lisieux fell to Edward III on that same day. He and his troops liked it here and didn't leave Normandy until they were driven out by the Black Plague of 1348. All this will be in my history of Mesnil."

She took a sip of her tea and looked at me happily, as if to measure my endurance, like an actress wondering if the moment had arrived when she'd do well to show a little leg.

"I have to admit, I never understood even one year out of the Hundred Years' War," I confessed. I offered her a little of the calvados I had found remaining after the O'Banyons' summer, but she had no need of it.

"You'll find the whole thing in my book, but from the point of view of Mesnil. During the second half of the fourteenth century, between a third and a half of Normandy died, what with the war and the *peste*. The population fell from a million two hundred down to six hundred thousand souls. If Mesnil had consisted of thirty hearths, it now dropped to fifteen—which meant there was a lot of wasteland between firesides. Then, in 1416, the year after the big win at Agincourt that made him a movie star, Henry V of England came."

"I'm with you now," I said. "But of course our reading of those events is all based on English propaganda."

"Right," Thérèse said. "Once more unto the breach: Olivier and Branagh and that Thompson woman doing her Inspector Clouseau imitation. Anyway, Henry V and his brother the Duke of Clarence landed near Deauville on Sunday, August first. By the next day—I'll remember it as your mother's birthday from now on—they were attacking the castle of Touques, and then Henry sent Clarence upriver along the same road on which Guillaume Apollinaire had his flat tire. They planned to winter in the area. Lisieux fell to Clarence on August fourth, and for the next thirty years, like the rest of Normandy, it was administered by a different pecking order because the top cock had been changed. Everyone was fine so long as they agreed with the new arrangement, did their jobs, and paid taxes to the new boys.

"Now this is interesting, and we're getting closer to Mesnil." She fished into her bag again and pulled out some notes to read from. "On February eighteenth of the next year, five months after the English landed, our enemy Henry V decreed that by the twenty-seventh of the same month, *'sub pena et periculo quod si quis eorum ad diem illum in domo sua hujus non inventus, extra protectionem nostram ponatur et tamquam brigans et inimicus noster teneatur et puniatur'*—meaning, essentially, that all who refused to return to their dwellings would be declared brigands and punished as such. The punishment for brigandage was death, as well as the confiscation of all worldly goods for the benefit of the offended party—i.e., Henry V. Some did not obey, of course, and the countryside was filled with looting bands of soldiers who had not been paid, and troublemakers, and Norman holdouts who took to the woods, leaving their homes and properties to the English or to other, collaborating—that is to say, 'obedient'—citizens."

I said, "You must write this book." I was thinking that one

happy thing about a book was that you could put it down after a few hours, or minutes. But then you would lose the passion in the author's delivery.

"So if you think of this as peaceful country," Thérèse said, "you must think again. Peace is a luxury we don't get very much of around here. Not in my history. Uprisings and wars of attrition finally drove the English out, but at considerable expense to us. Pont l'Evêque, held by the English but hard to defend, fell to the French in 1440, but only for long enough for the homes of the Anglophiles to be looted. Joan of Arc's infamous judge, Pierre Cauchon"—whose name rhymes with "pig"—"was made Bishop of Lisieux under the English, and his acquiescent administration was ruthless: it suppressed two uprisings during the troubles, in which thousands of persons from the countryside, branded as bandits because they disagreed with the invaders, were hanged and disemboweled, and their separated parts exhibited everywhere so as to encourage their neighbors."

Thérèse started putting her notes back into her bag and fidgeting, no doubt thinking of the next day's trip and her life class, maybe a new model to draw or paint. She stood and was about to leave when her eye fell on something else in her notes that she had to tell me about.

"I haven't found Mesnil mentioned in the records of properties transferred by confiscation during this period, but neighboring Blangy shows up often, as does Eparfontaines (now Fierville), three minutes down the road by car, where you remember the train used to stop." She pointed through my library to the south. "Look, in Fierville, in 1434, John Chamberlain, an English knight, was awarded in fief (meaning that he got to collect taxes on it and pay the next man up the line) land that had been confiscated from Guillaume le Gris (absent, and therefore disobedient), along with goods formerly in the possession of Raoul and Edmond de Tournay, knights, and other property that had belonged to Jacques Advisse, and to Jean Séguin, all of them absent and disobedient. He also received part of the heritage of Jean des Chesnes, knight, in the successions of his father and mother, as well as the goods of Jean le Forestier and his squire, who had been executed at Lisieux as 'adversaries of the king our lord.' By now our so-called king and lord was Henry VI of England, Henry V having died—a tragedy, according to the English and anyone else who lets Shakespeare be his guide to all this history. My own history of Mesnil will correct such misapprehensions. I have to go. I like to get to class first so I can pose the model."

We went downstairs and I helped Thérèse into her coat, thinking to myself, *She's worse than I am.* I was on the point of projecting that idea across the Atlantic toward my wife when I heard Julia's instant and obvious rejoinder: *Yeah, and nobody's trying to live with her.*

Thérèse took out a flashlight and walked twenty paces into the rainy darkness. Mme. Vera's lights were already extinguished, and only the small pool of light that fell from the dining-room window separated us from the Cretaceous.

"So don't think it's always been quiet like this," Thérèse called. "Not much, and not often, since the world began." She turned and came toward me again. "Nineteen forty-four would not have been the first time it made sense to hide the family and the cows in a cave within the commune of Mesnil. But I wouldn't know how to find that quarry," Thérèse told me. "If it's there."

FIFTEEN

Thérèse's passion for history put me to shame and reduced the scope of what I was occupied with to almost reasonable proportions. I always brought work with me, and the place was filled with its own projects, as well as the unfinished tasks of other people, and all of that suited me fine once I had adjusted to it— especially given the broader picture Thérèse had painted. But still, there were large, messy, and unexpected structural problems that I had to deal with quickly. That afternoon, after my shower, I had learned from Mme. Le Planquay that nothing could be done about the plumbing until two days later, when M. Le Planquay's people would start to replace the lead pipes in the *sous-sol,* reseal the wastepipe on the upstairs toilet, and, as a bonus, run a pipe for hot water from the electric tank into the downstairs bath so I could dispense once and for all with the propane lottery system. I was permitted to use the electricity in the meantime, she said, so long as I made sure that the hot-water tank was not empty. She suggested that I close the main valve in the downstairs kitchen and open it only when I must have water. So after Thérèse left, it was into a dry kitchen that I carried our teacups.

The telephone rang and "How is everything?" Julia asked.

"Beautiful," I said. *You know—with one thing and another and all.*

"And the house is clean, you said?" Julia continued. "You have water this time?"

"Plenty. Things all right there?"

"Good," she said, not stopping to answer my inquiry. "Because Margaret called. She and Ben are traveling in England with some friends. She wondered if anyone was in the house in Normandy, and if she could show it to Ben, and I said you'd love to have company. You're going to be there three or four more days, yes? What's the matter?"

"Rough spot on the satellite," I said.

"I thought you yelped and dropped something. Anyway, I think she said they'd arrive tomorrow night, and I told her there was plenty of room. What's wrong?"

I was in no condition to have guests. What was more, though there was nobody I would rather have a visit from than Margaret and Ben—old friends and pals and colleagues, people from whom I would normally have no secrets—I had inadvertently, a moment before, committed myself to not telling Julia about the state of the plumbing and the bathroom floor until some auspicious if undefined future moment, which plan Margaret and Ben were bound to preempt.

"What's wrong?" Julia repeated.

"Nothing. As Thoreau said, 'Simplify! Simplify!' I'll just gird my loins and go into bed-and-breakfast mode."

This, I should have remembered, was a sore point. American

friends, visiting us in couples during past summers and wearing different clothes each day, had sometimes looked speculatively at the wholly colorful situation of the house (and of their hosts) and seen the field as almost pure potential. Not only could we do this, and this, and this, they said, to make the house habitable (never mind that each "this" would cost at least twenty thousand dollars), but afterward we could run an outstanding bed-and-breakfast in the showplace that would result.

"Don't talk to me about B and B's," Julia said. "I'm just back from Waterville, Maine, helping Sally get material for her book. You'd be amazed, all these people who used to live in perfectly good cities going out to lonely but awful places and running bed-and-breakfasts. Waterville's got ten thousand people and there's nothing at all there except twelve B and B's and in every one of them the wives have left. Sally was so busy getting info for the book that she didn't even notice this interesting little social side-light. I mean," Julia emphasized darkly, "what can happen. In a lonely place.

"If either of us is going to do breakfast for anybody, it had damned well better be a friend, not somebody who thinks she is paying for the chance to express an opinion about the coffee. Friends like Margaret and Ben. They're good friends, and the only reason in the world I can think of at the moment to even consider having a great huge galumphing place on the other side of nowhere that we don't need is so our friends can visit."

I stood corrected.

SIXTEEN

I woke to thin rain falling against the slates and realized that I was to have four guests by evening: Margaret and Ben and their friends from Amsterdam. My situation could be funny only in a movie. Aside from stumbling onto big problems, I had got nothing done, and I had only a couple of days left here. The place was a shambles. Margaret had encountered the medieval comforts of the house when she visited many years before, so she knew basically what to expect—though the medieval quality of the comfort had increased dramatically with the recent collapse of the heating system and disappearance of the bathroom floor, the fact that running water was available only on demand, and my temporary bachelorhood.

The weather had changed: it was now as cold and wet outside as it was inside the house.

I must manufacture a speedy masquerade. Living alone, I had been camping, a concession both to my own inclination and to the state of the plumbing; I walked around wearing as many sweaters as I needed and did not care that it was cold. But now this had to seem like a house. I lay in bed, listening to the donkey singing from Mount Angel, and watching white clouds of condensation issue from my mouth as I breathed. I'd have to try to make them comfortable. The impending guests deserved meals that could be distinguished one from another, as well as sheets. Four guests would mean an aftermath of six to eight sheets in addition to mine, and four pillowcases, and four towels—all of which must be washed and persuaded to become dry before I would be free to go back to Paris. For the past several years in a row, I had been bringing quick-drying cotton sheets with me from home, since they were too expensive to buy in France. It came to me now that during my brief inventory of the linen closet the day before, in a quest driven from my mind since then by the state of the bathroom floor, I had noticed that these cotton sheets were the ones that had gone scarce or missing. I must therefore fall back on linen.

In 1968, and for a few years afterward, once we started returning regularly to the house, people from the countryside would appear at the door from time to time carrying household goods that they, or their parents, had removed from the house *pour la chère Madame Frieseke*, in order to preserve them during the war. We might be busy, say, putting glass into an attic window when there came a ring on the bell we'd hung outside the downstairs-kitchen door, announcing the arrival of a middle-aged man (sometimes with family), whom my mother (quickly snatching off her apron and putting on a kettle in the same motion) slowly recalled (with mutual tears) from a catechism class she had taught in 1935 to children in the village. He might have with him a china pitcher, or a teapot, or a long-handled copper saucepan.

It is always sort of hectic, Julia's mother wrote, *as friends keep*

dropping in and everyone has to go up to the salon and "causer"
[chat].

The memories brought back by these visits, mixed with gratitude, joy, concern, and the social burden of having to drop whatever was being repaired in order to respond to the bell—and to the news of deaths and marriages and births—could be quite wearing on my mother, the only one of us with any intimate emotional involvement with the callers. Plans for the day inevitably had to be jettisoned on such occasions, but there were ample compensations: among the treasures that reappeared this way were my grandmother's linen sheets, which for years remained the only ones in the house. They wore like wet iron, having been made to last the ages by my grandmother, who, when preparing her trousseau, had embroidered her maiden initials, S.O.B., into the pillowcases and roof-sized double-bed sheets, under the orders of the implacable nuns of the Visitation convent in Wheeling, West Virginia. The monogram branded the user.

Linen, like the bread of Paris, holds moisture well and is reluctant to part with it. Rain on a morning when guests loomed therefore caused me to recall, as I listened to the Angelus bells and delayed getting up, the bone-harrowing slide into chilled damp linen, as well as the nightmare battles waged in the name of getting the sheets dry.

For years the house had had no washing machine, and we still had no dryer. That was supposed to be the sun's job (or fault). Where my grandparents had employed people to beat the linen in the pond below the cider press and spread it on the grass to bleach and dry before they ironed it, our laundry days required the cooperation of at least three of our *own* number: one to wash, one to watch the weather, and one to rush out to the line in time to haul the sheets down before a spate of rain, and hang them up

Mme. Vera's as seen from the house (with laundry), 1995. Photo by author

again to wrest the most from any sun that appeared. The person who watched the weather—usually a child who had other business outside, like chasing chickens—also had to keep guard over the line, since hopeful calves would suck holes into the wet laundry.

Thus I started this day thinking dark housewifely thoughts. It was cold, dark, and familiar in the house. I put on sweaters and looked at the rain, which seemed impermanent somehow, a series of curtains spun of gauze or spiderweb filling the valley, showing no rifts. It could be like this for days. I listened awhile to the doves affirming bad news to each other in the eaves, then made coffee and sat in the dining room and let the BBC newscaster echo the doves while I looked out the window at the string of cattle ambling across the green slope between the cider press and the house, indifferent to the rain, eating as they walked. This was the Norman weather I'd expected. It, not the inside of a decaying house, was my real reason for being here—because, perversely enough, I loved this weather. It made the air active and the colors of the world defiant, and eliminated horizon lines right up to the windowsills. It forced plants to grow in a way that seemed preternatural. I'd found, for example, a limb cut off last summer by the O'Banyons from the plum tree that grew outside the guest room—a log thick as my thigh, just lying on the ground under the vanished lindens—putting out fresh new shoots and leaves this spring, even though, when I lifted it, there was no sign of its having bothered to send out roots. It was just continuing to do what it had always done, prompted by a climate that imposed life.

I had another cup of coffee and watched the rain some more, wondering how much of it was getting into the Mesnier-Bréards' masonry through the large opening I had noticed the day before in the wall facing the garden, from which it could easily work through the half-timbering and into the library, though not before rotting out the *colombages*. My breakfast table had filled with things I'd have to put away. Tonight we'd be five at table.

SEVENTEEN

One summer early in the sequence of our stays, Julia and I were in the house with two little ones, Christopher and Sadie. This was before the place had its first washing machine, which in many ways resembled the Citroën, and was bought used the first year France tested an atomic bomb in the Pacific. After the machine was installed, we listened to it for hours as it ground for forty-nine seconds in one direction, then paused balefully for exactly long enough to let you believe, *It's over,* before grinding back in the other. It was like climbing seventeen steps up and then either sixteen or eighteen down, backward. The only way to know for sure was to keep counting. "Perfect to wash Penelope's weaving in," Julia said.

Our friend Margaret's first visit to the house had antedated the arrival of the washing machine, and also our successful calculation of how many Pampers could be imported in one suitcase if they were deboxed and compressed like Wonder Bread. Expecting a homogeneous level of civilization in the West, we'd thought we could buy Pampers anywhere; we were surprised to learn that the only French answer to the disposable diaper was a nasty and instantly prebiodegradeable *couche* that teetered in an elastic belt. Julia, trained by the Madams of the Sacred Heart, claimed it was a mortification menstrual pad designed for nuns to wear under their hair shirts. An enterprising child such as Sadie could be kept in such a thing for less time than it took to disintegrate.

We were nervous about the bucket boiler, a galvanized percolator that had to be heaved onto the stove in the downstairs kitchen. We had purchased it from M. Thouroude's predecessor in the *quincaillerie,* but shied away from it because carrying buckets of boiling water with toddlers underfoot made us uneasy, though it did not faze them. We relied instead on hand-washing, of which I did not do my share.

Outside the house, the drive and pastures teemed with beasts. Twice daily, geese paraded past in a line with their young, the whole family shitting everywhere, in fat grassy greasy curlicues of the sulphurous yellow-green that the American painters used to call *merde d'oie.* Madeleine tells me the current name for the color in polite company is *caca d'oie.* At any rate, everything shat copiously outdoors: cows, goats, sheep, dogs, chickens, ducks. What the beasts of the field contributed soon became our problem as well when our own children slid in it.

That summer we were shaken by the loss of Christopher's large, black, motherly dog Duchesse, who wintered with Mme. Vera but rushed over to greet Christopher whenever we arrived. We were walking one evening along the tiny road at the foot of the property, in the direction of Mesnil, accompanied by Duchesse, when she was killed instantly by a car traveling at grotesque speed on a road barely wide enough for the passage of one car at a time. We were used to seeing the hedgerows bulge outward when the tankers shoved through in the evenings, after collecting the day's milk from the farms.

M. Tonnelier, the farmer (Mme. Vera's husband), buried Duchesse at the far end of the garden's first terrace. The loss of the dog proved how much danger there could be for our children on the road, and that realization was still fresh and raw among us an evening or two later when Margaret's daughter Millie arrived, humping a load not much smaller than herself. Millie had just finished high school. She had walked from the train station in Fierville carrying what she felt she needed for a two-month trek in Asia—Normandy being only her first stage. The train still stopped at Fierville then; if we wanted a day in Paris, we would start off at about four-thirty in the morning on the thirty-minute walk to the crossing, where we would flag the train. At the end of a long summer day—there would still be some daylight in the sky at eleven on the Feast of Saint John, the longest day of summer (June 21)—the walk back to the house was all uphill. It delighted us that the entire trip from Cambridge to Mesnil could be made using only public transportation and our legs. The Fierville station incorporated in its upper floor the residence of the stationmaster; the family's laundry hung from an upstairs window as Papa flagged trains below and Cécile and Pascal clamored at Maman within.

We'd known that Millie was coming, but not when she would arrive. The house had no telephone; all correspondence with the world was conducted by letter or through telegrams that the *facteur* brought up the driveway in his car, their wording inevitably having shifted in transit thanks to operators unfamiliar with the English language. These cables often caused us alarm but seldom provided any useful information. DOOM. COMNG. TROOBL.

still hard to get help in a house in which the kitchen was on the ground floor and the dining room on the first, the two being linked only by a narrow and treacherous inside staircase. Even for Parisian servants used to long corridors that accentuated the gulf between the classes of served (dining room) and servant (kitchen), this seemed too much. Therefore, the dumbwaiter was installed. It was an efficient contraption and survived the war better than much else in the house. How the imagined patrons of our never-to-happen B&B would have loved to watch Julia and me, their genial hostess and host, quaintly dragging their morning coffee to them on it, along with fresh flowers gathered from the garden while they slept! But Julia and I, as the perennial servants of our young family, had soon discovered that we had less use for the dumbwaiter than did the children who liked to ride it, and I tore it out, replacing its upper terminal in the butler's pantry with a small half-kitchen. This was the only kitchen we normally used unless there were numerous people in the house.

The laundry room had a cement sink running all the way down one side, designed to accommodate the wet part of the old cheese-making operation. It drained, like the kitchen sink, out a culvert under the driveway and into the fields. It was here that Julia was standing on the last morning of Margaret's visit, scrubbing diapers in a metal washtub balanced in the sink. The heavy wooden door to the outside was open to allow her to run out now and then into the pasture to test the intentions of the weather.

Margaret had taken Amos up the hill after breakfast to show him the woods and the view of the house from on high. They were about to drive to Paris, to fly to a place filled with romance, sun, comfort, and luxury: Provence, a part of the world where life was gay and carefree and nobody needed diapers. Amos went upstairs to pack while Margaret stood in the driveway to share a last gossip with Julia. Noticing the work-in-progress, she jock-eyed under her skirt, did that practiced feminine two-step shimmy, and tossed her underpants into the washpan. This was long before Madonna perfected the routine, a grand gesture of something like noblesse oblige, useful almost anywhere, and at almost any time, if the goal is to stop traffic.

"As long as you're at it anyway, you don't mind, do you, lovey?" Margaret said. "It's the funniest thing, but when I went to pack at home, I couldn't find a single extra pair."

As she and Amos drove away, Margaret rolled the elastic of her underpants up in the car window to hold them, fluttering, to dry *en volant*. Amos and Margaret looked a gallant, very on-the-road-to-Paris parade disappearing down the drive toward their eventual divorce.

Now, a week or so later, with the shadow of Duchesse's passing weighing heavy on us, Margaret's daughter Millie arrived and had to be *re*vived while the children, their faces white, were assured that the young woman was only indulging in a bit of self-expression and had not really died like their beloved dog.

Millie's trek was to take her through India, Nepal, Pakistan, and Afghanistan. She was convinced that though she planned to stay with friends, hardship and privation lay before her, and she must be self-sufficient. Her person-sized backpack was not large enough for everything she imagined she would need, so she was also festooned with baskets, valises, purses, and bags. We noted a square black wicker suitcase the size of a ham, with stiff round wooden oversized handles, which anyone who had ever traveled a block from home would have known could only be trouble. During the second day of Millie's visit, Julia began dropping hints about efficiency in packing, pointing out that if Millie intended to hike the mountains of Afghanistan, she should remember how she had felt after the two-mile climb from Fierville, and maybe carry less. "For instance," Julia asked, pointing out this most uselessly encumbering of Millie's containers, "what on earth is that black thing good for?"

"Underpants," Millie said. She was provisioned with seventeen pair she'd scavenged at home in the States. It was too late for the information to do her mother much good: the overflow joined the trunk of emergency clothes in the house. The black wicker object, too small for a picnic basket, too dumb for a suitcase, kicked around for the next dozen years until one day I had to award a prize to one of Margaret's visiting grandsons (Millie's nephew), who lugged it back to New York, a useful reminder never to win prizes.

EIGHTEEN

The jam closet could no longer be avoided. I had houseguests in my immediate future, as well as major construction pending in the upstairs bathroom, the floor of which was the jam closet's ceiling. The jam closet, like the bathroom, was three feet wide and about nine deep, filling the space between the stairs and the salon. The wastepipe from the leaking toilet ran through it. For years, it had been haunting me like the least examined of bad consciences.

Other than my frightening glimpse through the rotted bathroom floor, and its converse, that brief shuddering glance at the closet's ceiling, I had not really looked into it yet. Given the amount of dirt and rot that would inevitably accompany the labor as *torchis* and distressed joists came out, I knew I should clean the closet back to the bare walls—that is, if there *were* any walls. As long as it was raining, and since my time would soon be taken up by my role as host, I decided to use this morning for the job.

The closet had no door. Its opening next to the foot of the stairs was normally covered by a curtain, hung in such a way as to mask the stored materials as well as the wastepipe. Mercifully, the closet had no light. I had not seen the farthest reaches of the space since 1968, when, as Julia's mother had recounted in her letter, I retrieved the family's boxed books from friends, and from the attic, and built shelves everywhere in the house I could think of. What I had been unable to make shelves for had been stored either in the woodbox next to the dining-room fireplace or in the depths of the jam closet, on shelves where my grandmother's fabled jams had once been kept (blackberry and cherry from the woods; currant, gooseberry, apricot, and elderberry from her kitchen garden; plum from the tree that was still producing next to the house and whose cropped limb would not give up; pear and apple from the espaliered trees against the cider press; and wild strawberry). The more accessible environs of the jam closet had later become a repository for broken furniture and, in front of that, for gardening tools and odds and ends and other things that people like the O'Banyons had no use for. (It was not impossible that my tray would turn up there.)

The Friesekes had collected books seriously. My mother's mother's father, John Duross O'Bryan, who became somewhat wealthy from time to time, used to bring portions of his large family (there were eleven children, of whom seven lived) across the Atlantic from Philadelphia for extended stays. When he finally retired to Paris, in the 1890s, he brought his library with him. After he died suddenly of appendicitis in 1904, following an operation performed in the Paris apartment (at 206 Boulevard Raspail), his daughter Sarah, my grandmother, was able to commit her future to the fiscal risk at which he had demurred: she married an American artist. She did so, in fact, while still wear-

1
2
4

ing mourning; my grandmother was a determined individual. In due course many of her father's books came to the house in Normandy, including his collection of Shakespeare editions and books concerning the life of Napoleon; his *Lives of the Lord Chief Justices of England* (in twelve volumes), *Lives of the Saints* (in eighteen), and *Lives of the Queens of England* (fourteen); works in Greek and Latin; numerous volumes on Irish history and the "Irish problem" (O'Bryan having been a committed partisan); and Bancroft's *Works* and *History of the Civil War.*

Since I depend on books, I was curious to find out what had been consigned to this oubliette so many years ago. I hauled out tools and furniture and stored them in a dry part of the *cave,* and then, using a lamp on a long extension cord, learned with relief that the ceiling above the books was dry, whole, and free of mushrooms. I began pulling out books and stacking them on the stairs; as I stacked, I plotted the next oubliette, beside the attic stairway. (I had not been up to the attic yet.) Once up to my armpits in these books, I would, I knew, be a lost cause, and would simply disappear until something interrupted.

When we first unpacked the library, one of my goals was to keep its existential character. Those books that I found most curious or appropriate I put into the library: my grandfather Frieseke's books on fly fishing and bridge, his collection of humorous sketches, his Hazlitt, and his monographs on certain painters whose work he admired; my great-grandmother's tomes on domestic economy and the diseases of swine and poultry; my grandmother's volumes on gardening and porcelain, her Trollope and Scott, her W. H. Hudson, Lafcadio Hearn, and James Joyce; and my great-grandfather's Napoleon collection, which I consulted during the summer when I finally read *War and Peace,* shamed into it by Julia, who reread it every three years.

Second First Communion of Frances, 1925, at center, left of Frances, *l'abbé Quesnel, pastor of Mesnil.*

To unpack the jam closet was to entertain a jumble of family history, since in the days in 1968 when I had occupied myself with the obverse of this task, anything I had found sequestered in a book, whatever the thing and whatever the book, I had left exactly where it was, thinking the coincidence of book and thing and place a historical gesture that would be destroyed if those elements were to be separated. A paper tucked into a book, I felt, spoke of or to a person, place, and time we did not want to lose. Therefore, the holy card distributed at the time of my mother's second First Solemn Communion in 1925, for example, must stay between pages 72 and 73 of Stevenson's *Travels with a Donkey,* where it would edify, please, or surprise the next reader to come upon it.

As a matter of fact, my mother made three First Solemn Communions in Mesnil, under the direction of three large men in black robes, one spring after another, until she outgrew the dress. It was during the spring after the *third* that Lindbergh flew over. The theory in the parish was that children should be encouraged to keep participating in the rituals; but another, more important factor may have been that on account of poverty in the village, a girl's Communion dress might be her first and last real dress until she married. My mother's *first* First Holy Communion was commemorated in a photograph (tucked into a Philo Vance) taken after the occasion on the first terrace of the garden, in which were present, reading from right to left, my mother in her solemn dress; my grandmother and grandfather; Gayle and Mahdah Reddin (mother and daughter, Baha'is from Birmingham, Alabama, who stayed with the Friesekes long enough for my grandfather to paint a number of pictures of Mahdah); a woman I could not name; Germaine Pinchon, my mother's godmother, who rose early that morning with her mother (the next in line) to do the housework at their home in Les Authieux before the neighbors awoke. (M. Pinchon, at far left, enjoyed more success as a fly fisherman than as a painter, and Germaine and her mother were the only help the family could afford.) Next to Mme. Pinchon sat my grandmother's younger sister Janet, who studied voice all her life. In her youth she had to be accompanied to the singing teacher's in Paris by her sister Sadie, who acted as chaperon-interpreter and who treasured and often repeated the exasperated exclamation of the impresario: "Why could not God have had the kindness to place both the brain and the voice into one girl!?" Janet outdid even my grandmother when it came to risk in marriage, since the artist she chose to marry (also after her father died) was not only unsuc-

First First Communion of Frances, 1924.

cessful and faithless in matters of the heart, but also French, and Communist to boot.

Janet's marital selection made his living, from time to time, as the representative of a yogurt manufacturer. Speaking of help: one of my grandmother's tales, set in the period before Janet and Tonton improved their domestic arrangements by separating, had them throwing tomatoes at each other until the tomato supply was exhausted, at which point Janet gestured imperiously with a sweep of the arm that included the mess as well as the petrified servant girl, and commanded in a voice trained for the opera, "Clean that up."

Next to Aunt Janet in the late morning sunshine (I knew it was late morning because after noon the terrace would be shadowed

ing being. The problem with my approach was that the collection numbered more than six thousand volumes in all, some of which I had not laid eyes on since 1968. So on this rainy morning, I brought books out of the jam closet, brushed them off, and stacked them on the stairs or on the table in the dining room, looking into them only when I could not resist, and knowing that one day I must search, in an organized fashion, through every book in the house, to see what I had buried. Out of the jam closet came my great-grandfather O'Bryan's rhetoric textbooks, in Latin, from his time at Georgetown College; my mother's catechism texts; works by Hugh Miller and John Boyle O'Reilly; a vein of geology books from the 1860s; a 1949 (what stranger had left this here?) special issue of *Science et vie* on aviation, with breathless illustrated articles about the new generation of bombers and fighter planes; a set of Alpine guidebooks wrapped in a 1928 Paris newspaper filled with accounts of car accidents. (In 1928, the name of the day's saint was published in the paper's banner, next to the date.) I looked into one of O'Bryan's college texts and found its flyleaf decorated with a scurrilous little drawing accompanied by a brief lyric, describing "Brynie" standing at third base with his whiskers blowing in the wind, at what must have been almost the dawn of college baseball.

Further along, in a heavy volume by an American archbishop fulminating against the threat posed to the one true faith by public education, a slim white pamphlet caught my eye. A program for the 124th annual banquet of the Hibernian Society of Philadelphia, held at Doolan's Hotel on March 18, 1895, for the benefit of the Relief of Immigrants from Ireland, it provided the banquet's seating plan, a list of the society's honorable members, and the program of toasts. One of the presenters was John Duross O'Bryan, the text of whose "Ireland" was printed in the pamphlet. As to the gradual and unremitting incursion of the English into Ireland, he remarked (his words clearly balanced according to principles introduced by the Latin rhetorician at Georgetown),

> The usual became the lawful; and so the industries of Ireland, instead of flowing in channels that nature and economy alike, laid out for her peculiar interest, were, by legislation diverted into ways that drained her wealth into other coffers.

The dinner menu was also recorded: bluepoint oysters with celery (accompanied by sauternes); green turtle clear; Penobscot salmon, cucumbers, shrimp sauce, and potatoes château (accompanied by sherry); lobster cutlets; tendreté of venison, purée of fresh mushrooms, new potatoes, tomatoes farci, green peas (accompanied by champagne); terrapin comtesse; punch cruiskeen lawn; English snipe with lettuce; glaces, fruits, nuts, and cakes (accompanied by claret), and café noir and cognac.

If these people are coming tonight, I suppose I had better shop for groceries eventually, I told myself as I went into the jam closet to get another load of books.

NINETEEN

A telephone call from Margaret startled me out of my task. They were ahead of schedule and promised to be with me in time for lunch. I now had to drive to town and get supplies for lunch, and dinner, before everything closed.

On my way into Pont l'Evêque, I remembered the spectacle of Margaret and Julia at the sink. I had not yet tested the washing machine to see if it still worked. Sheets: I would have to lay out linen.

In Pont l'Evêque I noticed it was Sunday. Church bells banged in the rain and the streets bustled with crowds shopping for their noon dinner, which in these parts on a Sunday was a very serious affair. While shopping, I was conscious for the first time—no doubt because I was thinking in a proprietary way of the glimpse of "Old World charm" I was going to be able to offer Margaret and Ben—of the many rain-streaked posters in Pont l'Evêque in which persons of youth, nudity, and some beauty were exhibiting their sneakers. I realized how much during the time I had known the town, the provincial purity of the place had been dissipated by the incursion of urban culture. When we first came to Pont l'Evêque, there were no public images of undraped humans beyond a diagram in the window of the *pharmacie* having to do with trusses. Pont l'Evêque was, after all, the birthplace of Flaubert's mother and home of the same writer's blameless character Félicité, in *Un coeur simple.* No more than ten miles from the excesses of the beach at Deauville, it had nonetheless seemed a lifetime away; and Deauville was not yet a topless beach in 1968, nor would it be until long after the revolution.

Because of the rain, my car had to struggle for traction on the driveway coming home. Now one could stand in steady, declining mist and watch the approach of serious rain squalls, walking on wide legs between which might float snatches of clear sky as blue as the eye of God—but always somewhere else, across the valley. Normandy was Normandy again, a country made of rain. When the hill the house was on dried out during the summerlong drought of 1976, apple trees simply fell over because the earth they had stood in, having lost so much of its bulk (in the form of moisture), could no longer hold their roots. There was nothing to keep the orchards from giving in to gravity.

I stowed the groceries and surveyed the wreck that fate and I had been collaborating on in the situation room, formerly the dining room. In time for lunch, Margaret had said—so I'd take that as permission not to lay on a heavy spread at noon, as everyone else in Normandy was doing. That would give me time to hide the evidence of odd jobs and to get the place looking as good as possible. I wanted to do this partly because nobody could use the upstairs bathroom in its present state without risking sudden death, but mostly because I knew that Margaret and Julia had no secrets from each other, ever, and there was no way

Julia was *not* going to be talking at length with Margaret about my situation—and before I got home. I had already noted a tendency among women to agree on the (lack of) wisdom of taking on a second home in a foreign land: the men would always encourage, while the women would immediately and instinctively pull the long faces that might greet the news that we were about to have unexpected triplets on purpose now that our youngest was sixteen. *Women's sticking together,* I complained to myself, *is the curse that forms the cornerstone of civilization.* And you can't fool them, which is another way of saying the same thing. But you have to try, which accounts for the origin of language.

I rushed to find and hang curtains in the upstairs bedrooms—the fruit of a whole summer's labor on the part of Julia, my mother, Julia's mother, and assorted others—and then to reinforce the catwalk across the bathroom floor (Ben was a large and heavy man). I dusted the tops of furniture and put cloths across the most Victorian pieces from the O'Bryan line.

I heard my guests before I saw them, and saw them long before they managed to get their car to the top of the muddy slope. That gave me time to open the water main. The first out of the car was one I hadn't expected: Andalouse, a large unreconstructed French poodle of urban tastes who sniffed the falling air; declined to take in the riot of new experiences available to any dog arriving on a farm; refused even to acknowledge the frenzied greetings from Mme. Vera's yard; and instead stalked inside to seek out remnants of the scent of my mother's childhood pet, Chipette, also a poodle. Ben climbed out, loudly congratulating himself on getting the car up the hill, and then Teddy, whose head, since it reached almost to seven feet, I saw immediately would be in constant danger from ceiling beams and lin-

Chipette, ink drawing, F. C. Frieseke sketch book, 1936.

tels, and then Margaret. All wore sweaters and jeans and hats of one kind or another: they were fresh from a wet Channel crossing, and voluble about it.

Margaret stood in the rain grinning, and said into the car, to Ruth—the fifth member of their party—"I told you, just like Holland, except it's not flat, there's more rain, and everyone talks French except our host."

"We haven't come all the way to Normandy to take a nap," Ben said after lunch, as we gazed out the dining room's west window, overlooking the valley, at some little birds that I didn't remember from previous visits. They had been there for two days now, jerking up and down as if on strings, parallel to the slates on that face of the building; they seemed to be plucking out of the rain insects issuing either from the wall or from the *auvent* beneath the window. There was something both charming and worrying about the show, and Ben reinforced the latter quality by asking idly, "What's that they're eating? Termites?"

I'd looked up these birds earlier, while I was deliberating about my owl, and had decided they were a species of *bergeron-nettes*, yellow wagtails. I wondered myself what they were eating, inasmuch as it (or they) seemed to be coming out of the walls. As the resident expert, I must speak.

"The book says they eat flies," I temporized.

"Houseflies—that would make sense, coming out of the house," Ben said. "Anyway, I admit the weather's perfect for it, and I'm probably going to want to take a hundred naps while I'm here, but why don't we do something else today?"

Teddy and Ruth were knocking around the half-kitchen, doing the dishes. Teddy could barely make it under the ceiling beams without ducking. It turned out he was a paleontological biologist by trade. Ruth, closer to me in age than was Margaret, was rather small and energetic, almost haunted in appearance, and, I learned, labored under the cloud of an uncompleted Ph.D. thesis in anthropology, concerned with methods used to date the ancient human-worked flints that could be found in certain parts of Italy. Hearing this, I looked on her with an eye lustful with speculation, since the hill we were on was rich in flint, which often looked worked. Many a child of mine had returned to the house carrying a flint that either contained a fossil (or something that might become one given enough time or argument) or seemed likely once to have been used to skin a Neanderthal boar.

Ruth and Teddy discussed England and the English as Margaret kibitzed through the opening between dining room and kitchen, which under the present regime allowed diners and servants (who were now interchangeable) to converse and help each other.

"They're barbarians. That food! Wherever you go, the English try to give you a first course that's either a bad tomato or half an avocado stuffed with little canned shrimp in mayonnaise," Teddy was complaining.

"And you ask why England has remained an island!" Margaret proclaimed rhetorically. Her observations were often right on target, but they sometimes got her into trouble.

"I am now going to change into my warm clothes, which I am glad everyone warned me to bring," Ben said. "And then let's do something. Hit the beaches or whatever. According to the map, we're only about a dozen miles from Sword Beach."

"Get in the car and I'll show you around," I said. "I'll point out the way to the D-day beaches, and you can go there on your own later."

I drove my car, with Ben and the women in back and Teddy telescoped in beside me. Andalouse needed no persuasion to stay by the banked fire. I advised my passengers that they might have to walk when it came time for us to ascend the drive again.

Our road north toward Pont l'Evêque paralleled the railroad line along a short segment of the Vikings' river route through the Pays d'Auge, the valley of the Touques. From the backseat, Ruth informed us that this was the northwestern border of a carboniferous limestone deposit laid down in the secondary era in the region known broadly as Sedimentary Normandy—or, more euphoniously, since the Seine emptied through it, the Paris Basin. The exposed raised rock of Brittany was older, she said; granites and crystalline rocks made up the Armorican massif, whose northernmost protuberance, the Cotentin Peninsula, had been joined to southern England and Nova Scotia before those masses drifted off on their own—England because it insisted on serving avocado with prawns, and Nova Scotia perhaps to get as far as it could from England's diet. The Armorican massif, to the west of us, had formed a dike during the tertiary, when twice the Paris Basin had been flooded by shallow seas or lakes. The inhabitants of those waters had left chalk deposits hundreds of feet thick, above which were the flints generated by the decomposition of rock during the period of equatorial climate that preceded glaciation. Or so Ruth told us.

Perhaps Ruth should do the opening chapter of Thérèse's history of Mesnil, I thought. And Teddy could add a note concerning the area's ancient flora, the oldest surviving example of which was equisetum, or horsetail (a plant that looked as if it had been invented by Dr. Seuss), of which Teddy had already pointed out two species—one specializing in the field, and the other in marshy ground.

The hills rose on either side of the Touques Valley, all that was left of what had been a plateau of ancient ocean floor: islands of pasture, orchard, and woodland reaching as high as six hundred feet above what was now sea level, to which the myriad persistent rivers, streams, brooks, *douets*, and *becs* separating the peaks had washed their flinty beds.

"According to a friend of mine, Thérèse," I told them, "greatness has passed before us on this road. Louis XVI himself, in June of 1786, with a large and expensive retinue, followed this road. You must imagine the local folk filling the ditches with shouts of *vive le roi*, and now and then a brave farm wife rushing forward to kiss the hem of his carriage. The trip was sudden, and there'd been a frantic rebuilding of bridges and reinforcing of roadbeds. Louis was returning from the inspection of some absurd and absurdly expensive sunken fortifications he was building at Cherbourg against the English navy. He was heading, via Pont l'Evêque, for Honfleur and his beheading seven years later. Thérèse says Louis was warned before his trip, by his advance man, that because the Pays d'Auge country was remote, and its commerce required little in the way of cartage, he'd find many roads unfinished."

In fact they were still working on the stretch near Manneville.

We motored past fields and were still in fields when the town began. I drove my guests through Pont l'Evêque, dismissed by Louis XVI's scout as follows, "This little town has nothing remarkable." I tried for a tour that would mingle the historical with the practical, while mentioning items (such as Guillaume Apollinaire's flat tire) that should interest any tourist. The town stands at a confluence of rivers through or among or across which the Bishop (*évêque*) of Lisieux, within whose diocese the region fell, was said to have built a toll bridge (or *pont*—whose proceeds went, of course, to the bishop benefactor), during the eleventh century. I found it difficult to believe that the Romans did not have their own bridges long before that, but perhaps they made use of ferries. They could have collected their own tolls on those just as well.

Pont l'Evêque's coat of arms boasts two gold oxen on a red field. One rumor claims that the town's name had humbler origins as Pont-à-la-Vache, or Cowsbridge, easy enough to upgrade in French to Pont l'Evêque, or Bishopsbridge. The name does not turn up in the written record until 1077, the year Hugh, Bishop of Lisieux by right of consanguinity with William the Conqueror's family, collapsed on the road not far from where Apollinaire had *his* flat, in Ouilly le Vicomte. A *ouille* was a wine barrel in old French; in those days they still struggled to grow the grape in Normandy.

Lisieux had once been a walled and fortified city, but as Thérèse had told me, it was hard to credit Pont l'Evêque with the same. It sat on a broad, flat, marshy plain riddled with rivers: the Touques, the Calonne (which emptied into the Touques just north of the town), and the Yvie. I showed my passengers how the smaller, less trafficked of the roads from Lisieux toward the coast met Pont l'Evêque's main street, fumbled to maintain its direction, lasted another block, and finished abruptly in back of the jail and the glass-recycling bin, in a parking lot next to a long-unused covered *lavoir* that the Syndicat d'Initiative kept up as a monument to happy bygone times when women knelt and scrubbed. The other road, I explained, continued north from Pont l'Evêque and branched off to meet the coast at Honfleur and Deauville; that was the route along which Guillaume Apollinaire had driven, the route that Henry V's brother Clarence had followed on his way to take Lisieux, the route that

Lindbergh had later used as a map to guide him toward Paris from the coast, and that Louis XVI followed in the opposite direction, on his triumphal march.

Pont l'Evêque, having suffered its most recent truly serious battering in the religious wars of 1590 and having remained architecturally tranquil for the next 350 years, was practically obliterated during the liberation of 1944. Most of what was to be seen in Pont l'Evêque was therefore modern, apart from some sixteenth- or seventeenth-century remains. When the smoke cleared after the battle of Pont l'Evêque in August 1944, the thirteenth-century limestone church of Saint Michel was still standing, though it had lost its spire and all its glass. At the western end of the town (closest to Caen, the birthplace of Charlotte Corday), where some half-timbered sixteenth-century buildings had escaped the bombing, we got out of the car to wander. Swallows nesting in their crevices darted among the old houses and snatched insects from the streams and small canals they overhung. I pointed out one of the practical functions of the picturesque Renaissance style in which the second story juts out beyond the first: here, as elsewhere, these remnants of the *style ancien* had privy holes cut in the floor over the water.

Its being Sunday afternoon, and after lunch, and raining, Pont l'Evêque sagged in replete stupor. Shops that had flourished for trade that morning now looked abandoned and belligerently for sale. That would change the next day, I explained: Monday was market day.

I showed them Pont l'Evêque's hospital, the pharmacy, a shop where one could find a newspaper and another where one could not, two *quincailleries* (for hardware and bottled gas), a *droguerie* (for dry goods such as toilet paper, brooms, paint, steel wool, brushes of all sorts, turpentine to fill any bottle the customer supplied, mirrors, and toothbrushes), four bakeries, three charcuteries (for prepared meats or such cold dishes as celeriac or deviled eggs or crushed ham forced to look like a partridge, as well as cuts of meat whose country of origin was the pig), a shop for furniture, a shop for saddles, a shop for cloth, one for calvados, one for boots and shoes, another for clothes, three butchers, and two all-purpose grocery stores. Everything was closed up tight.

Ben, a generous and impulsive shopper when it came to supplying a friend's table, made impatient noises from the backseat. "Everything's closed! What about cheese?" he asked. "Aren't they supposed to have cheese?"

There was no shop for cheese alone, but I showed them a charcuterie where the next day, if they conferred with Madame, she would select for them a Pont l'Evêque (the cheese for which the town had been famous since the thirteenth century, though it used to be called Augelette) that would be ready to eat either then and there or on some future day of their choice. They could follow her progress and her muttering commentary as she tested each one with her thumb.

"If your will is perfection as well as conversation, that is the way to shop, as you know. I know that," Ben affirmed. "You say market day is tomorrow? We'll come in tomorrow and buy everything. Cheese and whatever else you want, we'll buy it, and maybe some other things as well."

Moved either by g⋯⋯⋯⋯n spirit of adventure, Margaret and ⋯⋯⋯⋯ger to go shopping next day, Monday—market day in ⋯⋯⋯que.

"The wine we had last night, was that something you particularly enjoy? or—well, we'll see what else they have," Ben said. He'd taken heed of everybody's warnings before heading to Europe and had supplied himself for the visit with large red flannel sleepwear, in which he was adding color to the breakfast table. He and Margaret and Teddy had been discussing whether or not they wanted to drive to the other side of Caen to find a village boasting a street called Place Donnelly, named after a friend of theirs who had brought one of Churchill's so-called amphibious tanks through the town (this one had floated, rather than sinking, like the first he commanded) during the liberation in 1944. But everyone was concluding that the best way to spend a rainy day in Normandy, aside from participating in market day, was in the solitude of the farm.

"It's seductive just sitting around this big house," Ruth said, "and figuring out what you should do with it."

The previous afternoon—because I myself hoped to sidestep this bit of local color this time, if I could—I had made a point of showing them the covered market in and outside of which organized gangs of competing farmers, shopkeepers, and traveling chair caners, clothes- and boot-sellers, florists, and merchants in trinkets once a week set up shop. The marketplace was off the main street, next to a small park edging one of the rivers, the Yvie, where men played *boules* unless it was raining very hard or there was something better to do. I had explained how when the circus was in town, the camels and llamas and elephants were staked out in this area under the poplar trees, to spend the day chewing and waiting for the evening's performance. All morning on market day the town would be bustling, and I generally tried to avoid coming in at all because even the quickest errands would take forever.

"It could be quite a mob," I warned. "But then again tomorrow, to make up for it, most everything will be closed."

Fortunately for me, the proposed excursion represented part of what my friends had come here for, and we sat around the table drinking coffee and making a list and watching the rain, listening to it drip from weak points in the gutters. Above us, the doves talked comfortably of doomed love.

Teddy and Ruth were turning out to be perfect guests because they were perfectly sympathetic: their house in Amsterdam, they said, was also falling down. "But with an old house, it takes a long, long time," Teddy consoled me. "Much longer than you have."

"I'm going to take a shower," Ruth called from upstairs. "Does somebody want to stand in that horrible closet underneath to catch me when I fall through?"

Friend looking out upstairs window, 1994. Photo S. Holstrom

"It worked for me," Teddy yelled up. "Just don't put both feet in the same place at the same time."

My guests were more eager for food adventures than their host, who kept worrying about the plumbing and wondering what bribe he might offer to prevent Margaret from telling his wife (and their absentee hostess), Julia, everything. Perhaps food would be the best approach? Could I confuse them by taking them to a restaurant in Deauville where they must study the menu and ask questions of the smirking waiter, such as "What is *verjus?*" My classical education, with detours down medieval alleys, had left me with a fleeting impression that in the fifteenth century, after the juice was pressed from the grape to foam into the beakers of the rich (having been transformed in God's good time into wine), the skins were soaked in water and the mess allowed to fester into a drink thought suitable for peasants;

somewhere between indifferent vinegar and dreadful wine, this was, I seemed to recall, called *verjus*. But if this was so, why would the tuxedoed waiter brag that the master chef, wearing his crown of Michelin stars, had been cooking his fish in it?

Julia and I always traveled poor, ever alert, especially when accompanied by children, to the virtues of bulk, simplicity, and value, and anxious that any foodstuff purchased should not present itself again immediately in the diaper. Our children consequently, once they became adults, felt they had been wronged; and some of our guests in Normandy may likewise have wondered why we came such a long way to put such unexotic things into our mouths. We forgot that for some people, cooking and eating were a form of entertainment, and that for others, more serious, closer to art.

When I was alone I thought in terms of meals that could be assembled in ten minutes and eaten in eight, with enough left over to fry or inundate with salad dressing for the next meal but one. And my expertise on wines might be called into question once I was seen contentedly drinking a glass of Château Intermarché with my canned mackerel and leftover-potato salad. Since I was often redolent of turpentine, it did not make a great deal of difference to my taste buds what I ate.

But I could rise to the culinary occasion if a bribe was called for. Here we were in Normandy, so my guests should be regaled with something Norman in the way of food. The advertised cuisine of the region depends heavily on cream, apples, cider, and calvados, this last being the epiphanic derivative of the hard, mean, green cider apples that are so dear to the cows, who trim the underneath planes of the orchard trees to precisely the tooth-grip reach of the longest-necked of their number. A whole school of nineteenth-century French painters based in Rouen celebrated this browsing gesture of the cow in heroic canvases. Calvados is a brandy with a good deal of character, especially when new, and many people dislike it. But if I wanted to cook something Norman, it should surely contain apples, butter, cream, and calvados—through which ingredients almost anyone should be able to walk a chicken, a potato, or a pastry crust with a reasonable expectation of getting a tasty outcome.

The Norman tradition of cooking is simply a variant of classic French cuisine, in which the aim is to mold as much fat as possible into a shape that will support the intrusion of some alien non-fat substance such as flour, sugar, or an exhibition of meat, vegetable, or fruit; the whole is then covered with a rich sauce (*sauce normande*, for example, is made from a base of cream and egg yolks). One can follow this basic plan and arrive at either stewed chicken or the Norman *tarte aux pommes*. My mother, when let loose in her Norman kitchen after thirty years of exile, proved to be a wizard at making the custards of her youth—even using the self-extinguishing gas stove that we cursed and did sentry duty over for many years until an engineer friend invented a valve to regulate the air flow and prevent us from filling the house with propane.

During one of the many summers we were together in large numbers in the house, we hired a woman from the area to come in once a week to help with the cleaning and do a bit of cooking. She arrived on her first day moving in a stately fashion with an odd muffled puttering sound that we understood only after she separated herself from the motorbike she had engulfed. Mme. Lecoq was a creature of Farouk-like proportions who subscribed to the old traditions. She produced a version of scalloped potatoes the very thought of which still causes my arteries to narrow: how so much cream and cheese and butter, all steaming hot, could manage to hold its shape, and how those elements maintained the illusion that potatoes and onions had been admitted to their company, we could not fathom. Julia and I did not attempt to duplicate such feats, a Puritanical awareness of the danger posed by saturated fats having intervened in the years since Mme. Lecoq's stint in our kitchen.

In the past, when Julia and I were alone with our children, we had often found ourselves feeling marooned in a Norman countryside flooded with things to eat. The cows groaned with rich milk and cream; they lay in their pastures, allowing the earth to support the burden of their heavy udders, and delivered them-

The dining room with Mrs. Frieseke, 1937. Photo Claude Giraud

selves of veal in their hours of repose. Apples fell from the trees and immediately began to exude cider. Wild rabbits were just starting to come back after their bad time with myxomatosis, so they were not eaten, but their comestible domestic brothers and sisters were raised in hutches outside farmhouses; one of the favored daily occupations of many old men, women, and children was to take baskets through the fields and roadside ditches and gather greens for the rabbits. In some butcher shops in Pont l'Evêque it was still the etiquette, left over from past days of privation, to present the otherwise naked body of a rabbit with its furry feet and long-eared head intact, so that the customer could be sure of not purchasing a cat.

A friend visiting from Italy would come back from the woods with delicious mushrooms that did not kill us. The hazel bushes provided nuts. Wild strawberries and blackberries, cherries and elderberries interposed themselves on the walks, and the children picked them. People fished the rivers for trout and salmon, and the nearby coast produced fish and shellfish in abundance. Our very young Christopher pulled snails from the tombstones in Mesnil's churchyard and tried to eat them raw. Veal, lamb, horse, pork, turkey, duck, goose, and guinea hen clamored for attention everywhere, whether on the hoof or in shop windows, where we could gaze on their complete displayed corpses or their intimate parts (the birds tucking their heads under their wings and laid out in flocks, the pigs' heads jolly with ivy wreaths and apples), or lovingly prepared roasts and scallops, or precooked and decorated individual portions ready-to-eat and looking like jewelry assembled for an African prince. All of that may have been fine for persons careless of the bottom line, but we were always getting by on an academic's salary, and Julia and I had to fall back on the countryside itself.

We had all the milk we wanted, from the farm; the children shook jars filled with cream until we had butter. Once Mme. Vera's garden was producing, there were shallots, onions, peas, beans, lettuce, potatoes, parsley, leeks, and so forth; and she sold us eggs that were perhaps freer in range than intended by the inventor of that term, who may not have envisioned the ovulating hen pecking at the severed head of a goat before the dogs could wrest it away from her, to tumble fighting down the hill into the marsh that used to be the horse pond, next to the bleaching field. The connection between mortal agony and the table was always intimately present on the farm, as in the restaurants in town (to which Julia's mother, a welcome visitor, sometimes took us). In Pont l'Evêque's Lion d'Or hotel, the trout offered on the dinner menu swam in a large tank that decorated the dining room, keeping fresh until the waiter netted it and whacked its head against a marble sideboard before carrying it to the chef. Even now, as we drank our coffee, I warned the shoppers, condemned rabbits, ducks, and chickens waited in the *marché* in Pont l'Evêque, trying to recall their prayers, crouched in baskets next to implacable farmwives who sat smiling at the deliberating crowd, holding their penknives ready at breast level, their little sharpening stones poised on knees gaily draped with flowered prints. It made the captive lettuces and fennels and creams and cheeses and pears and cockles and sausages seem equally alive in their baskets and trays, I told my guests: and similarly doomed.

TWENTY-ONE

Margaret and I, recalling her visit some years back, were agreeing that protein was a major consideration for the poor, among whom we included the budget traveler with children. Some of what seemed exotic to us in a cuisine such as China's in fact had to do with the ancestral scramble after protein: why else eat owl, or certain kinds of worms? Why else would snails, however attractive to a two-year-old, win pride of place on a nation's table?

Some years, after Julia and I had stretched our budget far enough to get the family to Normandy in the first place, there was not much left, and we settled down to a fare reminiscent of that enjoyed by fortunate peasant farmers in the Middle Ages—fortunate, that is, because it included milk and eggs in addition to cabbage and root vegetables and bread.

Once all Gaul was divided regionally into nine hundred jealous breads, just as it was into local wines (or beers or ciders) and cheeses. Each region had its own orders of ancillary fungi, specialists all. The cheese called Pont l'Evêque, under its old name Augelette, used to come in a variety of antic shapes including crescents and stars, as well as in the small square tile that was the sole remaining form the cheese now assumed under this name. It depended on a microbe native to Le Breuil en Auge, several kilometers distant from Mesnil—the same microbe of which the crevices of our downstairs kitchen harbored their own particular strain, which we could take advantage of whenever we wanted to make cottage cheese. My mother, who had been known, as I have said, to see things, claimed that in her youth she could pick up one of the cheeses curing in the cool room and watch its black mold climb from it onto her fingers and, heat-seeking, move slowly up her arm.

"So put cheese on the list," Ben said. "And bread. What kind of bread, and how much?"

The long, crusty, and nutritionally empty loaf called a baguette, designed primarily as an excuse for eating butter or as a sponge for sauce, was once only the regional bread of Paris. If well made, it is delicious within the first three hours of its baking, but it will not keep. Because it is photogenic and the press interfered, it is now known to Americans simply as "French bread," having elbowed its compatriot breads out of the footlights.

In Calvados the local (and sole available) bread in my grandparents' time was the *pain brié*. This was a dense, hard, salt-rising bread with a thick crust that had some of the virtue of kapok inasmuch as it resisted damp, its dough containing almost no air. After all, why should a Norman matron, careful with her money, buy air? If she wanted air, she could open her mouth and breathe, couldn't she? She didn't have to open her purse as well. *Pain brié* lasted, and it was good enough, especially when toasted, spread with butter, and sprinkled with salt (*pain brié, grillé et salé*). But it was out of favor now: few people bothered with it, tourists didn't know its name to ask for it, and some village bakeries in Calvados, the district in which Mesnil finds itself—its name hearkens to more spirituous matters— no longer even sold it. It was traditionally made in several shapes, among them the crown or *couronne* forbidden by the Germans during the war—whether because it was too frivolous or too patriotic, I could not say. In my grandparents' day, when there was no local alternative to *pain brié*, my grandmother was famous for her homemade American beaten biscuits. Our friend Charlotte, who was my mother's age and aunt to Thérèse, still mentioned my grandmother's biscuits (which she called *petits gateaux*) every time I saw her, with a nostalgia so poignant I feared she might be disappointed if Julia made a biscuit for her now.

"A lot of local color is just poverty," Margaret interjected as I was recounting my mother's tale of eating a meal at the house of a friend in Mesnil when she was a girl. After the main course was consumed, she remembered the plate's being wiped with a chunk of *pain brié* and the bread eaten before the dish was turned over and its underneath used for dessert, perhaps stewed pears with a dab of custard.

Julia's and my family's past diet of roots caused us to notice the protein existing all around us, profuse but for the most part unattainable. During one of our hungrier summers, a pig was butchered by the farmer, M. Tonnelier, providing a startling education for our children, whose faces were pressed against the library window thirty feet away.

Mme. Vera Tonnelier's father-in-law, M. Braye, lived in the second cottage on the farm, at the library end of the big house, which overlooked the part of the pasture where the butchering was done. He was the expert in charge. The occasion made for a family festival that included rowdy fun as well as labor. By the time we figured out what was happening, the animal was already hanging by its hind legs from the limb of a crooked apple tree, bleeding into a dishpan held by one of a group of women whose aprons and bare arms became bloodier and bloodier as the work proceeded. The dogs grinned, the ducks and geese gobbled in the bloody mud, hawks circled, and only the wood doves moaned—but they were always moaning. The beast was gutted, scalded, and shaved, and everything that had been inside it washed and picked over, sorted and saved. A small fire was kept burning, with the pot hung over it making the scene reminiscent of frontier life. Now and then something would be put into the pot or taken out. The majority of the carcass swung in the weather for most of a week, flanked by the tubs and the round crank-operated whetstone.

M. Braye's house, 1992. Photo Christine Livet

At the end of the week, with the butchering completed and the Tonneliers' dogs gamboling down the hill crazed with delight at the largesse of vertebrae that was finally rewarding their testy patience, M. Braye, accompanied by his dog—whom the children called "Frisky" Braye because of his abominably frank family approach to matters of mating—came to our kitchen door with one of his periodic gifts.

The dog's name may have been supplied by the children, but I later took impertinent delight in hearing that the natives of Frieseke's hometown, Owosso, Michigan, also pronounced *his* name that way. The alternate pronunciations I was accustomed to were, first, that used by the art dealers in New York, who conspire to call him Freeseekee, and, second, the way I myself was taught, Freesiku, which is closer to the way it would have been pronounced in Friesland.

"*Il n'est pas méchant,*" M. Braye always said, referring to Frisky Braye (meaning, "He's not dangerous": *chien méchant* is the French equivalent of our beware of the dog). When his (and Frisky's) business with us was completed, M. Braye would finally march off, shaking his head and muttering, to Frisky Braye, "*Ils ne comprennent pas*"—"They don't understand."

Since he and his wife lived on the place rent-free, being family of Vera's, he liked to make a gesture now and then. Mme. Braye stayed in the house and except at butchering time was visible only when she came out the front door and went around to the far side of their cottage, to what we later learned was their privy. Although they slept upstairs, in a room that could be reached only by way of an outside staircase, we never saw either one of the Brayes on those stairs. M. Braye was gardener for the château in Mesnil, toward which we saw him walk in the morning and after lunch, and from which he returned before lunch and in the evening, bent almost double over his stick. The flower garden in the enclosure around their house was breathtakingly lovely, a higgledy-piggledy hodgepodge of color that put yucca and bachelor's buttons side by side with lilac and floods of roses. By now the goats had got everything in M. Braye's vacant garden patch save for the lilac and a rosebush or two; the roses themselves were eaten as they budded.

M. Braye, while he lived, might turn up at the house one evening bearing branches loaded with cherries, broken from trees in the woods; or a bowl of blackberries; or flowers from his exuberant garden. This time Frisky was especially excited. The gift was a plastic plate covered with fat brown terete forms, intimate and slippery, which turned out to be the first example of black pudding we had ever tasted. We had seen this *boudin noir* being made under the apple tree but had not been able to isolate the nature of the product from the ferment of activity. The intestines had been emptied, trimmed, scraped, and washed, then stuffed with a mixture of pig's blood and flour, spiced in a way that my tongue no longer recalls because the commercial *boudin noir* I have eaten since includes cinnamon, and M. Braye's recipe dated from an epoch when a pinch of cinnamon was worth as much as a good hunting dog. With M. Braye's gift of blood sausage, we had a measure of protein for ourselves and our young. Like *boudin*, certain other staples in the French cuisine that we euphemistically call variety meats (sweetbread, tongue, kidneys, heart, liver, lungs, brains) were once simply those portions that were most available to the pocketbook, because they were less desirable than an identifiable chunk of muscle such as an *aloyau* (sirloin).

I did not want Margaret and Ben to have to go back home to Brooklyn and their dear deprived and say, "We stayed in a romantic if crumbling farmhouse in Normandy where we were afraid to use the bathroom and we ate turnips cooked six ways and it rained the whole time." So their first night I had served them *boudin noir* fried with apples and onions. This was a genuinely French dish, if not Norman; I got the recipe from Madeleine, my godson Gabriel's mother, who identified it as being Auvergnat, and thus native to the wrong part of the country—but under the circumstances, and on such short notice, I hoped it would take the place of local fare.

TWENTY-TWO

Everyone was being very kind about the water, which could be turned off inside the house, if not outside. It was raining and then clearing only enough to let us know that the sky was just taking a good breath before it started raining again. The birds and beasts outside passed through it all with indifference.

Ruth came down from her shower and gave me the all-clear to shut off the main and thus the gusher in the *cave* and the slower leak from the upstairs *cuvette*.

"Weather like this," Margaret said (she was wearing sweaters and a blue bathrobe of my grandfather's from the excess-clothing trunk, with heavy socks and slippers, but her breath steamed in the cold room like everyone else's), "and Nick's going on about the good old days of famine—well, it just makes me want to spend my whole day at the stove. That's what I'm going to do on my vacation." She was normally either in an office or making spot visits to evaluate day-care centers for the City of New

York—that was where she got her accurate view of poverty and local color. "Let's get something that takes forever to cook."

"Why don't you find a wild boar in the woods? Or there's tripe," I suggested. "As long as you're going to market, maybe you should add a few items to your list." And I told them, based on the version published by Alexandre Dumas, what they'd need to make one of the true specialties of the region, *tripe à la mode de Caen.* "Select one whole beef stomach, paunch and honeycomb; salt, pepper (we have that), and *quatre épices,* which is sometimes agreed to be a combination of pepper, cloves, nutmeg, and cinnamon; lean bacon; onions and carrots to slice; bouquet garni and garlic; twelve blanched mutton feet (which will result in three slow sheep who have confessed everything) and one boned calf's foot; a head of celery; twelve whole leeks; a bottle of white wine—pick up a white Château Intermarché, it's just as good as the red—and a glass of cognac (or maybe we could use cider in place of the wine, and calvados in place of the brandy; with what's left we'll have a *trou normand*)."

One didn't see them as often now, those large, square, red old men wearing bright working blue, who used to be the visible prop and support of every village; they had almost disappeared. Something had made them healthy and careful about their figures and modish in their clothing, or else they had died of apoplexy brought on by hard work, hard eating, and hard drinking. In the old days people would look upon one or another of such specimens, shake their heads, and predict, "Too bad, he will not survive the next feast of Saint Clair"—for in those days a feast was a serious event, lasting many hours and many courses, between which the famous *trou normand* (or "Norman hole," a fast gasp of calvados meant to revive the fainting digestive organs and trick them into wobbling into the next round) put many into permanent Norman holes, in the churchyards. The feast on the first day of Mme. Bovary's wedding went on for sixteen hours.

The Brothers of Charity of Mesnil were the remnant of an order established in the fourteenth century to provide Christian burial for indigents felled by the Black Plague; their members, all men, had sat apart in the choir of the church until the revolution (that is, the one led by Pope John XXIII, who forced the Mass into French and demanded the exchange of salutations among the congregation—which exchange we used, experiencing its reluctant execution, to refer to not as the "kiss" but as the "hiss of peace"—and mixed up the worshipers until there was no longer any perceptible difference between the classes or the sexes). For a feast held in 1867 to honor Saint Clair, the patron of Mesnil's chapter of the Frères de Charité (which then as always numbered fourteen men; the women who cooked were not expected at the table), the copious supplies ordered included ten pounds of stew beef, eight pounds of ground beef, an eight-pound sirloin, a nine- or ten-pound leg of mutton, two beef tongues, two rabbits, and thirty pounds of bread and ten of cake, as well as however much cider each man could offer up from his own cellar, and calvados produced for each household by the itinerant distiller.

"Anyway," I went on, "to get back to the recipe for tripe: we'll need two quarts of water, which I'll get by opening the main— that's easy—and eight ounces of beef marrow, which you'll want to add to your list. It cooks for thirteen hours. Does that sound about right?"

"Let them eat tripe," Ben almost quoted. He was a lawyer and a potter, and much as he respected and enjoyed process, there were limits. "You want tripe, we'll buy it ready-made."

A butcher shop in Pont l'Evêque sold the dish in the gelatinous state in which it was turned out by an establishment justly named La Tripe d'Or, or The Golden Tripe, because it had been awarded (twice) the gold medal for "*les meilleures tripes du monde.*" I myself was partial to tripe, but though *tripe à la mode de Caen* was one of the area's specialties, I had not served it the night before because I knew it was not universally loved, being often more honored in the breach than the observance. American guests who meet tripe for the first time at our table cannot fail to know they are somewhere other than home; many look with alarm at the folds and frills and deep-sea-seeming convolutions of these cuts of beef intestine and wish for something less like a child's nightmare of sex, and more like what they expect from a sedate French restaurant in the States: a neat portion complete with the accompaniment of a *coulis* and three perfect string beans julienned and laid out in a fan.

Still, I wanted to bribe my guests, and I was certain that would require more than my merely being the first one up so as to turn the water on and make coffee. "Get me a rabbit," I said. "You do whatever you want in my kitchen today, and tomorrow or the day after I'll roast you a rabbit."

Select a rabbit large enough to feed five. Ask the butcher to remove the head (which would discourage everybody) and to stuff the body with lean sausage, leaving the kidneys and the liver in the cavity. Ask him then to truss the corpse and wrap it in a caul. The cut ends of the legs, from which the *pattes* have been cleavered after everyone has agreed that the animal is not now and has never been a cat, will be sharp and should be padded with foil. Slide the prepared animal into a heavy plastic bag (which may or may not say on it *"Chez Lebon tout est bon"*). Pour into the bag some calvados, olive oil, black pepper, tarragon, powdered garlic, and mace. Suck all the air from the plastic bag (which the sharp edges of cut bone will not pierce since they are padded) and tie the neck of the bag with a rubber band. Leave in the refrigerator for a day or two or three, turning from time to time. Then roast the rabbit for as long as it takes.

As the others worked on making a list, Margaret went for inspiration to our small collection of cookbooks, but these came from my great-grandmother's years of running a large household outside Philadelphia, and they assumed a different world, one of breathtaking abundance. She consulted Alexandre Dumas's *Le Grand Dictionnaire de Cuisine,* from which we learned that in his time *verjus* had signified the juice of the green—that is, imma-ture—grape, pressed out and preserved in a sulfurated bottle with the aid of salt or vinegar. We had that much accomplished, but the morning was getting on. Teddy went outside to walk Andalouse, the one wearing boots and a yellow slicker and the other dressed in black absorbent fur.

"We could go out to eat," Ben proposed. Playing solitaire and looking comfortable, he was being polite rather than truly court-ing culture shock in the form of a French restaurant. "Whatever you want."

We had had guests whose pursuit of the stars in the Michelin red guide led them, like the wise men in the story, to Deauville or Honfleur or Le Breuil en Auge, where chef and *patron* were forever scheming to dazzle them by, as my friend Madeleine said (she was an excellent cook herself, and an excellent shopper also), "preparing things the long way: when they need melted chocolate, they shave it, rather than just dropping a hunk into a saucepan," she explained. And she swore that one could taste the difference.

I could suggest a country inn not ten minutes away that for all its recent upgrading still had a dining room decorated with curling strips of flypaper suspended above each table, and where the fare was a heart specialist's dream. The menu featured a three-course meal. The first course consisted of *rillettes*, a concoction of spiced lard containing strands of pork (like horsehair in *torchis*, to help it hold its shape), served in individual crocks and eaten with bread and pickles. This was followed by a three-egg omelette either *nature* (plain) or with Gruyère cheese. The third course was the *plateau de fromages*, which some thought best eaten with butter.

Or we could try the Hôtel de Bernay in Blangy. If it had been good enough for Dumas's Three Musketeers, who stopped there on their flight from Paris to the sea during the time of Richelieu (another item for Thérèse Chevalier's book?), it was probably good enough for us.

"I don't want to go out, I want to cook," Margaret called from the library, into which she had wandered. "That's exactly what I want. What's going on down the hill?"

We followed her into my bedroom and looked out the window at a white panel truck laboring to negotiate the last third of the driveway. It had managed the steepest and most rutted grade, under the trees, but then pooped out on the shallower slope of wet grass. We watched it back down a short distance and then try again, and fail. It backed out of sight under the chestnuts, and we heard it roaring to pick up speed until it lurched once again into sight and foundered anew on the wet surface.

"It's the plumbers," I said. I knew that truck, which had now backed down the driveway and disappeared again. We listened to confused vehicular activity. I saw Andalouse start loping down the pasture toward the commotion, with Teddy ambling behind her.

"They're giving up?" Ruth asked.

View from the library window. Pencil drawing, 1930, by F. C. Frieseke.

The wet air shook with a determined growl as the plumbers' truck lurched backward uphill and into view, gravel and chopped green spraying outward at its wheels until it sagged to a halt at about the spot where it had been making itself at home before.

"Plumbers get it up halfway," Margaret said.

"We'll make that line into a bumper sticker and try it in Brooklyn," Ben promised.

We watched the plumber's *gars'* assistant open the truck and pull out some lengths of copper pipe, which he shouldered and carried at a trot through the rain up to the house, past and among the cows that had been slowly gathering in the drive and pasture below M. Braye's.

I told my guests, "You go on to market and enjoy yourselves. Get me a rabbit. I'll stay and play with the plumbers."

TWENTY-THREE

Teddy had brought his boots from Amsterdam. "I always travel with them," he said. Ben had managed to find some that more or less fit him at the Intermarché during the morning's expedition; I had mine, and the house supply provided for the women. The group having decided that the best response to the weather was denial, and the house in any case having become a playground for plumbers, we resolved to adjourn outdoors after lunch.

"We noticed trees downed here and there on the property," Teddy said, "Andalouse and I, roaming this morning. If you'd like, we could cut some wood. Where do you get your wood supply?"

"From the same people who take care of the fences," I told him. "I think it's part of the deal."

"Then we'll cut some, just in case," Teddy said. But he was overruled: the consensus was that we should walk in the woods and not plan to do any useful exercise.

"Hedonism's where it's at," Margaret announced. "Hedonism

minceur." She had returned from market with turkey thighs cut crossways, and before lunch she and Ruth had made a flurry of cutting and peeling onions, carrots, celery, and other vegetables, casting them into a pot, and starting what Margaret claimed would become, after hours of slow simmering, a sort of turkey osso buco. That would struggle in the downstairs kitchen while we were out getting some hedonistic exercise in the weather.

The rain appeared to be thinning toward a hesitation, which fooled no one. We put on slickers with hoods and set off uphill, with Andalouse and Teddy in the lead, into the woods called, on old maps, the Bois du Loup Pendu, or Wood of the Hanged Wolf.

Frances and her mother, one afternoon long years ago, were looking for some cows that had last been seen wandering toward

F. C. Frieseke, The Fountain, *oil on canvas, 20 × 24 inches, 1923. Private collection.*

these woods. They climbed the steep stairs leading from one flourishing garden terrace to another and arrived at the overgrown parkland at the crest of the hill, which was bounded by the alley of lindens. Fred was painting on the second level, and it must have been going well, since they could hear him singing.

Frances and her mother were through the park and well into the older wilderness of woodland, past the linden alley, before Frances thought to remark, "I don't remember that maze from before."

"What maze?"

"The maze we just went through."

Her mother said what mothers say to children who have seen something that isn't there, but she allowed Frances to convince her to backtrack and look where they had been, if only to demonstrate that there was nothing there. Nothing like a maze now, or indeed then—though years later, when for some reason they had occasion to look over the plans of the grounds designed by Mesnier while he was redoing the interior, they found that they called for a boxwood maze, of which nothing existed save for the ghost that my mother, holding a wand with which to herd the stray cows, had walked through that day, calling "Blanche, Pascale, Mireille, Désirée."

As Thérèse would no doubt have enjoyed explaining to us, the enormous forest extending inland from the coast, of which this area was a part, had once belonged to the king of France and was held in fief to him by the Duke of Normandy, and then in fief to the duke by the Viscount of Auge, who was, in the eleventh century, a member of the Bertram family: barons of Bricquebec, with large holdings on this side of the Touques and fortified seats not only at Bricquebec but also about eight miles from Mesnil, at Fauguernon. The forest's wealth was fenced in for the benefit of its owners, and named after the River Touques. One of its cantons (or large divisions) was known as Loup Pendu, and our neck of the woods was still known under that name in the seventeenth century.

The last wolf known to have been killed in Normandy died in 1868, and since then they have been extinct in the province. However, in its place names, the region abounds in wolves: Canteleu and Canteloup are both variants of Chanteloup (Wolfsong), of which there are five examples in Calvados, in addition to three St. Loups (a Christian appropriation of an old pagan divinity), a Louvetot, and two Louvières (Place of Wolves). A look at a 1:25,000 map of our area turns up a Camplou, a Bonneville la Louvet, a Chemin de la Mare aux Loups (Track of Wolfmere or, maybe better, Wolfmere Drive), another Rue aux Loups, and Les Louteries. (Lieu Loutrel, for its part, refers not to the wolf but to the otters, or loutres, that used to be fished out of the streams with long barbed forks until they were eradicated.) In terms of wolf names, the charmingly christened Lieu d'Amour (Place of Love—there must be a story!) is no less surrounded by menacing predators than is La Taupe (The Mole), its neighbor.

If the wolves are gone, moles are still numerous in woods and fields, and occasionally on walks I have come upon dozens of their little dead bodies lying beside the path. Not so long ago, one of the forest-based livelihoods practiced in the region was that of *taupier* (moler), whose practitioners traveled through the countryside in large wooden casks or hogsheads on wheels—perhaps containing in their fragrant interiors Mme. le Taupier and the blind little ones—the whole contraption dragged by mules. The *taupier*'s *métier* was to trap and kill moles and, for all

I know, skin them and sell their hides. (In the thirteen hundreds, the fee for trapping 130 mature moles was the same as that earned for hanging a person—about a week's wages for a watchman. This fact goes some way toward explaining the relative merits of various portions of the rural economy; it is also the kind of information that likes to accumulate on my dining-room table and then move into the library when guests come, to build up on the floor next to my desk, on which I usually have my detailed map spread out to help me locate something.)

The forest's old ways still showed on the map. Because of the availability of fuel, numerous places were named La Forge, for the forges in which bog iron was once worked into ingots. The people of the woods also made glass and gathered the bark of trees to sell; Ecorcheville, or Barkville, was not far away. Bark stripped from felled oaks was used for tanning leather, the procedure for which constituted a major source of the pollution that accompanied eleventh-century industry. Its acids fed into such rivers as the Ante below Falaise, where Duke Robert the Devil (known to his friends as Robert the Magnificent) found Arlette bathing and quickly promoted her in rank from daughter of Fulbert the Tanner (known to some as Fulbert the Embalmer) to mother of William the Bastard (known to *his* many friends as William the Conqueror, Duke of Normandy, and King of England).

TWENTY-FOUR

Setting out, we skirted the ruins of the garden's terraces by way of the pasture in back of Mme. Vera's and ducked under the strands of rusty barbed wire looping unconvincingly along the trunks of the large and ancient lindens and beeches that marked the boundary of the forest. Underfoot were the husks of beech-nuts, browsed through by deer or boar over the previous fall and winter. The undergrowth was wet and yellow-green, confused by a jealous riot of competing sprigs and runners. It smelled like a change of world as sudden and absolute as the step across the line between pasture and town.

Originally a forest denoted a place with a boundary that was meant to keep the people out and the wild animals *in* for the recreational hunting of the owning class. The people of the coun-tryside were effectively trapped within the areas of cultivation, beyond whose boundaries they could trespass only within strict limitations and on peril of their lives if they were caught poach-ing protein. The larger *forêt*, like the smaller *breuil* (as in Le

Breuil en Auge, which is situated next to a thicket of remnants still on the map under the name Le Bois du Roi), signified a preserve, "in the old and long tradition still honored by the Sierra Club," as Ben remarked, climbing in boots that were already proving too small, "by which the fortunate sought to preserve the benefits of the wilderness for their own exercise and moral uplift, and to keep it safe from other people who might defile it by using its wealth to offset their hunger. And in

The garden stairs, 1995. Photo by author

France, I have to say, one gets the sense of an uncanny social order. For example, landing at Cherbourg and waiting for our car . . ."

Our path was thick with wet *fougères*, or bracken—large, rank ferns already almost waist-high. The woods, only sporadically cleared—this part most recently by us, some twenty years before, to provide capital for the new roof—had a piebald look. Some of the pines we had planted in place of what we sold were still struggling aloft, but for the most part the native growth was deciduous: chestnut, horse chestnut, oak, linden, sycamore, and ash, with an occasional accent of dense green from a box or holly.

Long-lasting, slow-growing, and evergreen, these last were often used as boundary markers for woodland lots. Now and again we saw a matched pair of gateposts lost in undergrowth, or caught glimpses of the shallow quarry or overgrown cart tracks.

Ben continued, "We were standing there waiting, in that place where the passengers get off the boat, and we noticed the crowd parting toward us as if it were these ferns with a wind blowing through them. Nobody seemed upset or even particularly preoccupied by whatever it was that was causing the movement; they all just went on chatting or scolding or reading their papers or jockeying for the best places in line. When our section of the crowd opened up, we saw a small parade: five uniformed police officers, two women and three men, one of them handcuffed to a well-dressed middle-aged man who was carrying a briefcase. Except for the crowd's moving to make room, it was as if it were not even happening. The police and their captive marched through without looking to either side, though the shackled man smiled in a way that one might read as shamefaced, maybe nervous. After they passed, everyone fell back into the opening they had made and continued their business. We may have been the only people at the station who noticed."

I showed my guests the linden alley, which led from woods to woods in a stretch only as long as the long side of the house, itself not visible from this height. The linden alley was a folly, meant merely for decoration since it was too narrow to accommodate a cart and, in any case, had never gone anywhere. It was planted as a place to walk in. From here, when the trees had lost their leaves, one could look down and see the face of the house that the Mesnier-Bréards had done in masonry: white tinted by lichen to a warm yellow, with insets of floral garlands under the upstairs windows. This day we argued about whether or not we

The front of the house from the third terrace, 1937. Photo Claude Giraud

could actually see the smoke from our dining room, which would
be joined in that chimney by the smoke from the bedroom Ben
and Margaret were using. Birds darted through the wet space
under the lindens; beyond the alley, the unused quarry was
already thick with blackberry brambles flowering in their ram-
bunctious version of the rose. In that area, where we had done
extensive clearing, doomed birches and alders sought to take
over, but they were soft and temporary and would be shaded out
with time, once the serious hardwoods could establish themselves.

Our path through the woods was an old one, the equivalent in
French terms of a British footpath. After giving onto the abandoned quarry at the top of the hill in back of the linden alley, it
skirted the backsides of a sequence of farms on one side, keeping to woods on the other while never surrendering its quality of
always seeming poised to offer insight into the forest primeval.

The front of the house from the top of the hill, 1995. Photo by author

We had brought sticks with us to beat our way through the bracken, and to break the backs of the blackberry canes that sought to take advantage of the path's offered access to the sky by snaking across it at eye or ankle level. Andalouse the city dog kept to the path immediately ahead of us and neither looked nor sniffed to left or right. The haze of brilliant damp that struggled to magnify the secluded sun rendered the colors vivid and vibrant, and I would have thought the same to be true of the smells, which should have provoked desire in any dog. The woods harbored foxes, several varieties of weasel, badgers, deer, and wild boar in addition to smaller fare.

It seemed to me that the songbirds were more plentiful each year; I did not recall having heard about any deer when we first came back, but these, too, had become progressively less timid recently. I suspected that the region was now producing fewer young men with the skill or patience to hunt these enemies of agriculture, and that the more people's livelihoods depended on things they could do in town without getting dirty, the better it was for the deer.

"That sounds just like a cuckoo," Margaret said.

The first time we traveled through Tuscany, Julia and I had noticed that the shapes of the landscape, and of individual trees or rocks within it, proved something that had never before occurred to us: such artists as the Sienese painters of the fifteenth century had been reporting, not inventing, an organization of landscape that we, foreigners both in time and in geography, had dismissed as the kind of fake for which the faddish term of the day was "magical."

Likewise, what does the American do about the cuckoo, on arriving in a land in which that bird's voice is such a common-place as, after a while, not even to be noticed? A person of Margaret's age, if educated in a certain way, would be familiar with the repeated musical descending minor third in a hundred familiar warhorses of European origin, from Respighi back through Beethoven's Fifth to a song by some composer in the Middle Ages whose name has long since fallen off his work. The cuckoo supplied the metaphor for a joke (about husbands' losing the attention of their wives) that was making people yawn generations before Shakespeare. The familiar references in English literature, if piled on the unfamiliar ones, and those in turn on top of references drawn from other European languages, would make a tower higher than the embarrassed cuckoo could ascend attempting to escape them. The cuckoo sings only in May. Overfamiliar as a cultural footnote relentlessly repeated, the song, when it first occurred to her ear for real while we were trudging through the woods, was simply a revelation to Margaret: she exclaimed, surprised with pleasure, "God! It's all true!?"

It was the sort of delight that nothing could be done about afterward, however, because we were strangers in the bird's country and to refer to it in a familiar way would have seemed like dropping, in conversation, the wrong nickname for a famous person we didn't know.

"Must be," I told Margaret. I hadn't heard it, though I'd been hearing it for days; that made it familiar, if not exactly mine: I could not use it in Cambridge.

So we walked along the muddy path, beating back ferns and breathing in the complex forest odors that Andalouse disdained, and we were accompanied by the nagging of cuckoos and the blackbirds' extraordinarily intelligent musical approximation of spirited if polite conversation between rival women, and only the crows sounded like home—in fact, like taxi drivers, Margaret said. She understood them as easily as if they had been growling in Brooklyn, "Get a move on, lady," or "You call that a tip?"

I was keeping an eye on Ruth, hoping to see her stoop and pick up a flint on one of whose raggedy faceted sides she would show us evidence of Cro-Magnon human workmanship, perhaps pronouncing it "not of museum quality" before tossing it into the brambles.

The remains of this ancient forest—of which not a single stick was ancient, the woods having been farmed and exploited for a thousand years—occupied the whole crest of the hill, spreading over several hundred acres. This part of Europe had been pretty much forested out, and a good hardwood trunk—such as an oak—was still of such value that after felling a tree, a lumber-jack was required to stamp an inventory number into the fresh cut, so that each trunk could be registered and accounted for.

Because of its scarcity, much that in the States is commonly made of wood (such as popsicle sticks, fence posts, and tooth-picks) appears in France in the same shapes but made of plastic or cement. And as for things manufactured from wood pulp, such as paper plates and napkins, when American friends coming over to visit asked us what they should bring (perhaps meaning what outfits?), we used to tell them, "Bring paper plates and nap-kins." In France we could not afford them.

Wood was used sparingly in building here on account of expense—another reason I had slowed down when I was build-ing bookshelves. Our friend Suzette, when she came to visit Julia and me in Cambridge, believed herself to be on the American frontier: "All those trees everywhere in the streets and gardens!" she'd exclaimed. "And the dwellings!"—she gestured toward the clapboard houses on our street—"Everyone lives in a log cabin!"

We reached the spot where the path widened to become a cart track and we no longer had to go in single file, far enough apart to avoid being lashed by recoiling branches. I started noticing that the farm buildings we were passing, from which an inquiring dog emerged now and again, were no longer the comfortable, run-down affairs I had been used to. More and more they were being spruced up, leaving our tumbledown wreck looking very much the outsider. Even the cows appeared more prosperous and better educated than those on my side of the hill. (Perhaps they aspired to the *première qualité;* they walked more daintily and lay with more conviction and less abandon, seeming to be vegetarians by choice, unlike the cattle that haunted my fields.)

From the road along the crest of the hill we could look out through orchard and across the valley of the *douet* and see the village of Mesnil, mostly redbrick from this vantage point, and dominated by the church tower. Mist bulged in ragged racing scraps between us and the town, with pods of rain battering it down now and then to allow us a vista.

Ruth hung back to talk to me, her red coat pattering with earnest rain. "I'll tell you what to do," she said. "And what you should tell Julia. I've given it a lot of thought. That place of yours is perfect for a B and B. Teddy can give you advice since he knows construction; he's done so much with our place in Amsterdam. Of course he says your wiring is all shot, and you don't want to take many chances with that since it's all two-twenty, but after you fix that, and maybe get some real beds—not to imply that what we're in isn't comfortable, Teddy and I, but if you want people to pay real money for a nice experience, it can't just be a mattress on the floor that makes you bump your head on the sink whenever you get up. And that room off the driveway that you call the *cave*, where there's the biggest leak—that's pretty much wasted, right? You could put a bedroom in there, though you'd have to put in a floor first, but it has water already—I know, a sauna!"

"How much will you take to make sure Ruth never runs into Julia?" I asked Margaret. I'd been gently, over the last day, trying to coax Margaret into my camp.

"No, really," Ruth said. "And about the bathrooms . . ."

I'd had more or less the same conversation with my friend Madeleine in Paris on my way out here. I had offered Madeleine and her family the use of the house whenever they liked, since it was more convenient for them than for me, but Madeleine knew country houses. By the time you arrived for the weekend and cleaned everything enough to be able to stay there, she said, it was time to start cleaning in preparation for leaving; the men never helped; and you had to take clean sheets from the city and bring them back dirty to wash once you got home (something she always does when they come to visit us in Normandy, I should add; this is standard French etiquette when visiting friends with second houses in the country).

Madeleine's preference, shared by the rest of her family, was to have an efficient apartment in Paris and to travel wherever they could, whenever they could, staying in hotels. What fun would it be, she asked, to visit the house without us? No, if they wanted to see that part of the country, they could find a hotel in Deauville. But thank you.

Madeleine had come back to the apartment from her office to have lunch with me, and I had told her what point Julia and I had reached in our continuing argument. Since she and Tom had known the house in Mesnil for most of the time we had been using it, Madeleine was full of suggestions, not least among which was, "Why are you even *thinking* of doing this? It's so much to keep clean." Even though she has spent a great deal of her life with Americans, Madeleine has never got the idea that one can both enjoy something and fail to keep it clean.

We sat in her living room looking at her view of the Eiffel Tower as she described a collection of chrome fixtures she had bought, but not used, when she was redecorating her apartment's bathroom in marble. These would be expensive for us to buy again in France, and unwieldy to bring from the U.S.—such things as toilet-paper dispensers. Madeleine reminded me that we had in our two bathrooms nothing but little wooden boxes screwed to the wall, intended for the old French prewar *imperméable*-style folded brown squares. She had been brooding about these boxes, on which our habit was to let the rolls of toilet paper perch on end, like pink attendant birds. She insisted, as she did every year, that the place could never be rented to French people, who looked for cleanliness as well as comfort when in vacation mode, and for whom the charm of rusticity did not encompass an aura of dilapidation. For many of these, she repeated, the concepts of cleanliness and comfort were indistinguishable.

Madeleine, like Julia, had an intimate knowledge of the house's potential charms and horrors, as well as an interest in the overall puzzle: How could we make it work? Especially given that we had little money to invest and must rely instead upon the strength or charm of our personality.

"Why don't you take the money and use it in small amounts to go to India and Croatia and Australia or Morocco?" Madeleine asked. (*Or throw it all in a hole?* Julia did not ask, but she was thinking along those lines.)

Why did Ruth, like every other American who came to visit, look over our potential predicament and immediately think of institutionalizing it as a bed-and-breakfast?

"You women hang together, don't you?" I complained to Ruth as I beat the bejesus out of a blackberry cane. Ruth fell silent, studying all the ways I could ruin my life and hopes and marriage in one fell swoop. From across the green Atlantic (gray on this coast and at this latitude) I heard Julia talking in firm, if negative, solidarity with her sisters, *Not to mention the things I can't stand to think about, like flying and plumbing, how do we make it nice? I don't know what to do with that house to break it up. It's three squat railroad trains going nowhere, one on top of another, and a roof, and the bottom one half -buried; and how are we going to get light into the place with those beautiful paneled solid doors to the garden that let no light in but plenty of wind? How can we work on it faster than physics and neglect are working against us? And then there're the two cottages, and what do we do with the ruin of the cider press? And everywhere on the place the piles of rusting machinery, and bottles, and the rest; we don't even know what everything is, or where it is. And the garden—the garden . . .*

"The main thing is a dishwasher," Ruth said, her mind at peace. "People nowadays want that. But I don't see where you'd put it. The upstairs kitchen is impossible, and the one downstairs is worse."

TWENTY-FIVE

Are you painting?" Ben asked. He'd noticed my canvas and supplies heaped in the library, waiting to be put away. He was sympathetic; his own hands were itching because they had been too long away from clay.

"Not this trip," I said. "I only have a couple of days, and besides—"

"I like seeing your paintings all around the house," Ben said. "There's a lot of wall left . . . and I know you. You're like me; we have to work."

"Yes, but to make more art one has to be a criminal optimist. And at the moment . . ."

Talking later over Margaret's turkey osso buco in the rain (but the rain outside, and we inside, and the plumbers long gone), we darted around a variety of subjects in a postmodern frame of reference (which frame Julia was always trying to explain to me and I kept failing to understand).

"We have to see the town of Mesnil," Margaret said. "And I have to say something to Mrs. Frieseke. Your grandmother. Something that's between the two of us."

Margaret had known that lady well, and part of the draw of the house for her, as for me, was the continued presence in it of my grandmother, whom she had never called anything other than Mrs. Frieseke.

"She once told me," Margaret confided, "speaking of you, Nick, and I quote: 'The woman he marries is going to have to love him an awful lot.' "

"I guess what you should really do is restore the whole thing to the way it was," Ruth suggested, opening a bottle of red-with-a-label that Ben had selected in Pont l'Evêque.

Teddy coughed. "You'd have to know not just construction but theater to make *that* happen. Besides, if you look at it from here, it never was what it was. Memory creates, just like history. Unless you have a really good fossil record."

We listened to the rain and tried collectively to imagine the establishment as it would have been seventy years before, when the Friesekes were living here. I pulled out a letter begun but neither completed nor sent back to Owosso, Michigan, by a visitor in 1925, which I had left within reach, together with the book it was hidden in—a prize awarded to Aunt Janet for stocking darning—after clearing out the jam closet two days before.

July 23

. . . to Lisieux, where Mrs. Frieseke met us. She was all in white, with lavender velvet ribbon, [illeg.] *a wicker* [illeg.], ["Has anyone noticed a large wicker tray, while wandering through the house?" I asked. All shook their heads] *and wore smoked amber beads.*

1
8
3

*She is tall with fine brown eyes and so vivacious and welcomed us
so warmly saying Fred F. was so excited for two months that we
were coming . . . a drive six and a half miles to their farm in the
country . . . has barns,* [illeg.; carriage house?], *springhouse and
dairy,* [illeg.] *and picturesque studio are the buildings scattered
around. It is hilly like Sadie's Pennsylvania hills, and wooded like
Mr. F.'s Michigan woods. Little Frances F. is ten, a sweet, winsome
child, with blue eyes, two braids of brown hair. She is fair with
turned-up nose. She has a little friend from Paris, Marcelle Joli,
spending the summer with her. She has a tutor each morning*
["The schoolteacher from Mesnil," I explained. "He would have
been available during the summer"] *and practices her piano. Fred
has just finished a large picture of his daughter seated at her own
piano in her bedroom by her open window. She has so many rabbits—and a white spitz dog* [this was Wicky, who came before
Chipette the poodle]. *Their house is old, with scenic paper on*

1
8
4

F. C. Frieseke, The Practice Hour, *oil on canvas, 26 × 32 inches, 1926.
Private collection.*

*Excursion to Deauville, 1919. (*Left to right, *Dr. and Mrs. Hally-Smith, Frances, Suzanne Hally-Smith, the Friesekes.)*

walls—a library, dining room (was the kitchen) with its open fire-place and copper kettles—dresser, charcoal stove and china closet (like wardrobe) oak dining table—timbered—every floor red tile—dumb elevator from kitchen downstairs, next living room with scenic paper very old, old piano, vases . . . lunch served by two maids in pleated white aprons and black dresses. Their own cider like champagne, and Bordeaux wine—tomato salad and egg; egg soufflé and sliced ham; [illeg.] *lamb, potatoes, carrots, beets, beans, peas (garnished) and* [illeg.] *vegetable dish; Romaine salad and pressed* [illeg.] *in loaf and sliced; fancy French sweets, fruit etc.; coffee in the library. Afterwards we walked about the place taking pictures—the cider mill was interesting, also the springhouse and pool—and the studio most of all. . . . We drove to Deauville, a famous watering place, and* [illeg.] *Back 11:30.**

*Adapted from the diary of Mrs. Fred B. Woodard of Owosso, Michigan.

"The photograph of the group at Deauville, then—that's these visitors from the Midwest?"

"No, that's the dentist, Hally-Smith, and his family. I gather the Deauville run was a regular part of the routine for visitors. Marcelle, the girl who was here to play with Frances, was a Fresh Air kid from Paris. There were Americans visiting all the time. The painter George Biddle and his wife, Jane Belo, were in at the beginning, before the days of plumbing, even. When the Frieselkes first bought this place of medieval comfort but more-than-Victorian splendor, they had to make use of the fields when nature called, and Jane Belo later said, 'I've known that house from the thistle to the pull chain.' William Glackens and his wife and children came, and family or friends of the family from the States who were making the tour. Then, too, since they were so far out in the country, if Frieseke was painting someone on commission—a child's portrait, for example—my grandmother had to put the family up for the duration. So Stellita Stapleton, when she was standing in the garden holding her head still as she tried to blow gnats off her nose, had a mother not far off needing tea and sheets and lunch and her turn in a bathtub she could get to without balancing across a catwalk. The William Preston Harrisons of Los Angeles came with their little boy, who borrowed one of Frances's multitude of rabbits to hold while he was having his portrait done in the salon. They needed those two maids, and the cook, and Georges the Russian chauffeur—"

"That's what I was saying," Ruth chimed in, gathering plates. "It's exactly the perfect situation for a bed-and-breakfast."

The rain poured down; there was just enough wind to rattle the slates and shutters. We broached the calvados, and something brought the conversation around to the theme of ruination.

We argued about the wreckage of war in terms of cost: the billions of dollars' worth of junk abandoned in the deserts of Iraq and Kuwait; the "amphibious" tanks still rusting in the gray salt water off Omaha and Sword, Utah and Juno beaches, their canvas skirts long melted away; the floating cement harbors (codenamed Mulberries) that were uniquely designed and made and towed and positioned as part of the invasion's supply line—at what enormous expense!—and one of them was instantly destroyed by a freak storm. Thinking of the abandoned hulks of cars left to disintegrate at the bottom of our pasture, of the roofless cider press, and of the vanished and vanishing outbuildings, I found it easy to extrapolate to those other fortunes lost through war, the monuments to private industry quickly depreciated from the credit to the debit column.

The argument tried to veer toward the sentimental, toward a gauzy nostalgia for the good old days of chivalry—until I recalled Thérèse's telling me that in the days of William the Bastard's conquest of England (he sailed from Dives, a harbor only thirty miles from Mesnil, with 880 troop ships carrying sixty thousand soldiers, and other transport), a good suit of mail (with the rings welded) was worth as much as a small farm, and that the full equipment cost of the average armed knight, complete with horse, was equivalent to about three big expensive cars today. In terms of national treasure lost, then, and individual fortunes blasted away forever, not to mention dead people, the wreckage left behind the Conqueror's successful action could fairly be compared to the smoking ruin made of Normandy's cities in 1944, or, more recently, the destruction wrought in Bosnia or Kuwait.

"And yet it all looks so friendly on the Bayeux tapestry," Margaret said. "So friendly and so—so *doable*."

"Do you remember Christopher on my shoulders, when we walked after dinner that first summer and he talked with the owls?" I asked Julia when she telephoned in the middle of our late calvados. I figured she must be lonesome for the place and the occasion. She should be part of this.

On those lambent evenings, with their varying press of slow diners left in the house, Julia and I had often escaped to walk outdoors in the dusk, reaffirming the start of our own family. Dusk fell late in July and August; unless you were in deep woods, you could still see your way at ten-thirty. The moment we stepped out of the house, we'd see the bats swooping in swags out of the attic to hunt the moths that battered against windows lighted with kerosene lanterns, or Normandy's pallid and impotent mosquitoes. Owls hooted, and Christopher hooted back in a wistful, earnest, and amazingly skilled response that brought the real birds closer for a silent, circling look. The cows kept eating wherever they stood or ambled, in pastures that sprouted heavy dew as soon as the sun got low enough to let that happen; or else it was gently raining.

"Never mind the *petitio ad feminam*—in other words, can the sentiment," Julia said, hearing me coming a mile away. "These phone calls are expensive. I'm just making sure Margaret and Ben got there safely, and that they're comfortable. I am their hostess, after all. And as far as Christopher goes, your son's been after me all day. He's on your side and wants to do you a favor by persuading me we have to buy. He took me to lunch to lay out his new plan for how to turn a Norman farm to fun and profit."

I braced myself to hear again the reasons for us not to run a bed-and-breakfast. Teddy selected a log from the woodbox and put it on the fire. It hissed, since he'd cut it in the rain during the late afternoon, feeling impatient with the wait inside for dinner. Andalouse, lying next to the fire, groaned with pleasure.

"Did he feed you Chinese?" I asked Julia in as speedily noncommittal a change of subject as I could come up with on such short notice.

"A fish farm," Julia said. "He wants to flood my one piece of flatland—that marshy place between the *douet* and the road where we noticed the poplars were down last year, and where the cows always find mud to roll in—and raise trout there. He's drawing up plans for interconnecting pools and dams and wants you to make him a map."

She paused.

"He claims there's a better future raising fish in Normandy than there is in computers," Julia pushed on, relentless as the rain.

She paused again.

"At least he'd be allowed to eat his clients," I pointed out.

"Speaking of eating clients, let me talk to Margaret," Julia said. "You found them sheets and everything? Are they having a good time?"

The rain poured down.

Ben pulled out his deck of cards and started dealing bridge hands. With Margaret on the phone, we were only four; Ruth was my partner. Despite the fire, the room was well ventilated, the draft under the dining-room door keeping the room's air from becoming what a person might call close. Since I was trying to overhear Margaret's side of the conversation in order to infer Julia's, I played an indifferent hand. The scraps I overheard from Margaret were not completely promising.

"Why don't you just think of it as his mistress? . . . I know, well, yes, that's a good point, a mistress he'd try to keep secret from you, which would be an advantage to you, and she'd cost less to keep up. . . . No, no, the airplane trip was awful, worst ever—bumpy? at least a dozen times I thought we were going to ditch. . . . Yes, he put flowers in the rooms, he's really putting on the dog. Flowers in the rooms, and we're making sure he eats. . . . Fish farm! A fish farm? Of course . . . exactly! . . . exactly! . . . It's what I've always said: if there's anything harder on a marriage than children, it's men . . . exactly!"

I realized that my partner had become the dummy, which made me the responsible hand in a five-heart bid I did not recall initiating. Adjusting my snooping to spring to full alert only if the word *bathroom* should be mentioned, I turned my concentration to the game.

TWENTY-SIX

I was wakened at four in the morning by the furious, shocking beauty of a nightingale's song under my window, and the answer of another nightingale not far off. I could hear, under the birds' sliding chuckle (which had always seemed sinister to me), the rain still falling out there. The singing of the nightingales (whose principal *nourriture* was spiders) brought back a buried memory (unless I made it up, or unless she did, but maybe it was true) of my mother's saying that her tutor, M. Letellier, had told her seventy years before that in his youth, "There were always nightingales in your woods. Often I used to stop my horse so I could listen to them, driving to my home from the station at Fierville."

After sleeping and waking again, I found the experience in my more recent memory both so real and so unusual—I had not heard a nightingale for fifteen years—that it seemed the kind of thing that must in prudence be dismissed as mythological or, as the dictionary would put it, merely *poetical* and *obsolete*.

As much a glad surprise as any nightingale, M. Joffroy

Frances with M. Letellier, the schoolmaster of Mesnil, ca. 1923.

knocked at the dining-room door early in the morning as I was pouring coffee for Ruth and waiting for M. Le Planquay's *gars* and his assistant, a first-year apprentice. They had at least another full day's work, maybe two.

M. Joffroy did not come inside but stood out in the rain, smiling and pointing at the side of the house, so that I had to step into the garden to see what was pleasing him. He was a tall man. He wore a soft cloth cap but otherwise defied the rain, sporting a white shirt and a blue sweater that shed water. His gesture tricked me into the yard, where we shook hands and he pointed at the sight that had caused his delight. On the telephone wire drooping from the cracked and yellowing stucco of the wall, two large snails were making what must for them be passionate love.

M. Joffroy kissed the pursed fingers of his right hand and flicked a blessing from them into the universe. His eyes danced. "*Escargots de Bourgogne.* Very rare in these parts," he exclaimed. "People have eaten them all."

"They're all over the property," I told him. Only the day

before, we had remarked on the exuberant population of sala-manders, snails, and slugs—the fat orange ones that bask out in the open when it rains, taking in the moisture like topless bathers at Deauville absorbing sun.

"And soon there will be more of them," M. Joffroy said, his voice filled with approval at the couple's endeavor. "You will have all the snails you want."

Preparing snails gathered in the wild, I happened to know from reading up on them once in the strangely titled (at least if one thought about it from the point of view of the snails) *Joy of Cooking*, required starving them for ten days in a covered basket in a cool place like my *cave* and then feeding them new lettuce leaves each day for two weeks—a process designed to detoxify them in case they had been in pasture on such poisons as the leaves of the foxglove (digitalis) that now blasted color into my dining room. Then they must be boiled for an extended period of time—days, maybe—and forked out of their shells, to have their innards cut out and then matched with their weight in minced gar-lic and three times their weight in butter before their emptied and enhanced black bodies were packed back into their shells to bake.

"It's one advantage of keeping the place so run down," M. Joffroy admitted. "The *escargots de Bourgogne* have almost dis-appeared elsewhere. I suppose we could think of this, what you're doing here"—his gesture included much of which I was ashamed—"as ecology."

We'll suggest a snail farm to Julia, I thought. *Since she doesn't like the sound of fish. Christopher might go for it; he likes process—and snails, too,* I remembered. The ancient Romans used to grow them on ranches, feeding them sweet bay leaves and wine. Christopher, who would eat anything that crawled, especially in the shallow parts of the sea, always called them "land snails" to distinguish them from the periwinkles he brought home in quantities from the mudflats of Deauville.

As was the custom in the country, everyone at the table rose and shook hands before M. Joffroy and I settled down to business. Alerted both by me and by M. Le Planquay, M. Joffroy had come to survey the damage in the upstairs bathroom. I followed him up the grand staircase. The son of a farmer, born in a village six miles away, M. Joffroy was skilled at reconciling the habits of the countryside to the expectations of foreigners. His sense of humor triumphed over my indifferent French, and therefore we communicated rather well; he served as an invaluable aide whenever I needed to confer with craftsmen.

At the top of the stairs, he peered around the corner into the bathroom and shuddered. "That's dangerous," he told me. "The floor is gone. A thing like that, it always makes me nervous. I think"—and here he acted the part of someone sitting on the toilet and beginning an unexpected long fall into a bottomless septic tank—"I think with your permission I will not go in."

We stood together at the top of the stairs while he deliberated.

"You want a mason," M. Joffroy said.

In France, at least in the countryside, the forms of manual labor comprising the building and repair trades are clearly and carefully delineated, even though in my experience most workmen can do a bit of everything. During the great drought of 1976, when the hills turned almost orange, making Normandy look unexpectedly like Cézanne country, we upgraded M. Braye's cottage by putting in water and a toilet (what did Aunt Janet use when she stayed in that house? I wondered), an installation that required the contributions of three separate and independent specialists: a plumber, a mason, and a *terassier*, or digger, whose job it was to make a hole for the *fosse septique* (septic tank) in earth that had hardened to cement. That summer we finally understood the advantage of our thick mud walls, which always kept the inside of the house cool and damp, even when the temperature outside soared over the hundred-degree mark for rainless days on end. The *terassier,* retired from the bureau of Ponts et Chaussées (Bridges and Roads) hacked away in the blazing sun day after day, relying only on his shovel and quantities of Negrita rum. Each day we saw less of him, until he was at last consumed by the perfect hole he had made in front of M. Braye's yucca.

As we passed through the dining room again, M. Joffroy looked at Ben's and Teddy's bulk with respectful wonder and shook his head. "Having no floor, it makes me very nervous," he said. "And Madame Julia, your wife, is well?"

Alert and suspicious, I refrained from saying.

"I will find you a mason," M. Joffroy said. "The place is rented for August? Then perhaps we should have the mason come right away if he is free, though in the summer . . ."

He went out by the door into the garden, and I watched through the window as he stood and wished the snails success in their efforts to bring back the glorious population of that fabled era of tranquillity, then went around the house to his car.

"Julia didn't seem at all discouraged by the state of the bathroom," Margaret said. "In any case, she didn't mention it last night on the phone."

"Ah, well," I said. Trying an evasive tactic, I suggested, "It's perfect weather to walk to town."

"You mean you didn't tell her?" Margaret was not to be distracted.

"I like a *fait accompli*," I said. "Or if I don't really like one, at least I prefer it to the alternative."

Teddy had already marched off into the woods carrying a saw. Ben's feet, having risen in protest against the boots he had bought at the Intermarché, elected to keep him at his solitaire, accompanied by the tintinnabulation of the plumbers downstairs, while the rest of us strolled forth.

Ben said to me as we left by way of the garden (where the coupling snails were still as heedless of their audience, Ruth claimed, as actors in some of the live shows in Amsterdam), "The point is not what it *was* but what it *is*, that's my advice; and not what it *is*, but what it's *going to be*. The future. The present is already gone." He was talking either about gambling at solitaire playing by Vegas rules, or about my concentrating a major part of my life's attention on a farm on the far side of the ocean from home—I wasn't quite sure which.

The effect suggested by the morning's weather was not so much rain as a stingy underwater tour. We had planned to cut across the pastures and through Mme. Vera's courtyard, but as we reached the driveway we heard a shot, a hoarse cry, and then another shot, and Mme. Vera rounded the back of the thatched garage carrying a rifle, with a red shawl thrown over her flowered dress, and a man's hat on her head to keep the wave in her hair from being ruined by the rain.

All three of us had jumped, first at the shots and then at the sight of Mme. Vera, armed and dangerous. She leaned her rifle under the thatch and attacked us with kisses, ignoring the disquiet of my guests.

She told Margaret and Ruth, "*C'est un gros renard* [a big fox]. You heard him barking last night? Coming for my chickens—I missed him."

That was the cry we had heard after the first shot—Mme. Vera's fury at missing her target. She pointed up the hill to the stooping branches of beech trees marking the edge of woods and pasture. "He's gone now," Mme. Vera said, acting the part of a successful fox hightailing it into cover. We had to stop so Margaret, who had spent some time with Mme. Vera in the past, could visit with her as she began feeding her chickens. No animal in history had ever been less interested in chickens than was Andalouse, who waded through them as they screamed and stuttered, refusing even to notice them or acknowledge that they were in her way.

"Like Marie Antoinette among the common folk," Ruth said, gesturing toward her oblivious bitch. "Before her last encounter with them in the Place de la Concorde."

Wafts and wefts and waifs of mist fled toward and past us through the rain and made everything greener. Mme. Vera began explaining to Margaret and Ruth about the cows' being struck recently by lightning, and about the attendant shortage of sugar.

"And you were here during the war?" Ruth asked. "Right here, on the farm?" Mme. Vera spread her arms, speechless, indicating, *What choice did I have?*

"It is so good to see smoke in your chimney," Mme. Vera said as we turned downhill. She acted the part of smoke rising into rain, looking supple and transient.

We waded across the next pasture, dodging glutinous *bouses de vache* (cow pies) reconstituted by the rain, and climbed a padlocked wooden gate to join the road at the compound, a group of two cottages and a converted *pressoir*, or cider press. One of these, loaned to my family by Tante Margot Lafontaine, was the cottage where we'd first stayed in 1968, when we started working on the house.

TWENTY-SEVEN

Once upon a time," I told Margaret and Ruth, "Mesnil was inhabited by a group of sisters, all of my grandmother's generation, and all as devoted to her as she was to them. And they in turn were succeeded by their daughters, all of my mother's generation, and all of them equally devoted to each other. Yes, there were and are men here and there in the family, but it always seemed to be the females we encountered, and certainly the females who endured; and we always thought of them under their family name, Lafontaine, even when they'd been separated from that name for generations.

"Suzette, roughly my mother's age, danced with her in a fairy costume in the garden when they were six and ten. She's the weaver who organized the rug in the salon, and who used to live year-round on the hill on the other side of the valley, in a *chaumière* that I'll show you on our way back. She's moved to the Loiret now and complains that the white cows that look into her windows there are strangers. She once made a pilgrimage to

Frances with Suzette performing in the garden, ca. 1925.

Jerusalem, to promote friendship between Muslim, Jew, and Christian, walking all the way from Mesnil with her suitcase in a wheelbarrow, each night negotiating a place to sleep in whatever house she came to, where she would deliver her message of peace. She was one of about a dozen in that family. Julia is a genius at this and could tell you all their names, and many of their stories—whom they married, where, and when, and the names of their children.

"The remade *pressoir* belongs to Suzette's sister Charlotte, who loves the memory of my grandmother's biscuits and comes every summer from the south with her children, some married and with their own children. The Lafontaines bought as many houses as they could in the *commune,* and kept them in the family."

This group of three buildings, all vacant at the moment, had been inhabited when we first arrived in 1968; in the one on the right were two friends of the Lafontaine family, Mme. Rohe, a widow who was a painter, and Mlle. Gabry, a retired nurse who, like Mme. Rohe, had been captured, tortured, and incarcerated by the Germans during the war for their part in an underground radio operation in Paris. Eventually they had escaped from the prison where they were being held, and had made their way to freedom. I had never heard the whole story, and never from their own mouths, but they were now both dead. Their *chaumière*, of the half-timbered construction shared by all three buildings, was surrounded by flowers.

During that summer of 1968, we had been overwhelmed by the warmth of the welcome given us by these old friends, and friends of friends, of my mother's family, whose intimate attachment resumed as if there had been no break at all. It was, though, a bewildering lot of people. They spilled out across the countryside and met us unexpectedly at the market—and we wanted desperately to remember which was which. Julia's mother, writing home to a friend after a party at the house shared by Mme. Rohe and Mlle. Gabry, described one afternoon that year:

August 18, night

I think I told you there was an open house Saturday afternoon. This is the first day I wore slacks. Not having time to come back to my hotel and change I ended wearing a dress of Frances'. The party was about 75 people including Xopher [Christopher, then two]. *House is next to Tante Margot's where they* [i.e., the Kilmers, when we first arrived] *lived and adorable. Two ladies who have fixed it up. They were both in slacks! Anything you wanted to drink including scotch. Glasses had piece of tape with a number— an idea worth trying at home. There must have been 20 varieties of food passed, from tidbits like cheese, olives, sausages, to four kinds of sandwiches, teeny croissants, I couldn't tell you how many kinds of tarts and cakes.*

Hopeless to figure out people but there was a nucleus I knew.

*Two who spoke English well. One married to an American Colonel
who is visiting her mother. Other is maybe going to be my prize for
Christy Cleland* [another story]. *Thérèse Chevalier who teaches at
Oxford but this year will be doing something in Lille two days a
week and will have an apt. in Paris. She is simply a dear and so
are her father and mother. He is Maurice Chevalier even to his joie
de vivre.*

*Xopher had a field day. I think he will be a playboy. Said he
liked the party because all the ladies kissed him.*

*The real Kilmer touch to me is that yesterday they had a piano
delivered but we haul chairs up and down stairs for meals. Very
late souper last night of soup, salad, cheese, fruit and bread pudding with framboise, and almost 11:00 before I got back.*

Charlotte's place, the redone *pressoir*, was on our left. Having
been speculating, on the other side of the Atlantic, about our
own *pressoir*, I studied it with a keen eye but could see no way to
make our ruin (which was much larger) anything like it.
Charlotte's was charming and comfortable and not in the least
industrial-looking. Farthest from the road, in the center of the
group of buildings, was the cottage of Tante Margot Lafontaine,
a *célibataire* (spinster) of my grandparents' generation, which
had accommodated the whole batch of us when we first
arrived—Julia and I along with Christopher, my parents, five of
my much younger siblings, and a nephew-cousin-grandchild.

Julia, writing home earlier that summer in a stage of the campaign that would bring her mother to join us at arm's length, had
described our living conditions within the broader context of
Mesnil as we waited to get into the house, and then just after we
moved in. The pleasures and dismays that are her reward for
possessing acute powers of observation have stayed with her
and, if anything, increased over the intervening years.

The Lafontaines own the whole area. There are about 100 of them. When Mama [Frances] *was growing up there was just the main house, big with outhouses etc., but rather ugly, being Victorian. I have just seen it, not been inside. Mama says it is beautiful. Anyway, the family had ten children or so and have continued.*

Actually Margot Lafontaine is single. Quite a few of the women around here are; Mama says it is because of the war taking so many men. All the people we meet have been affected directly by the war, the least being that their houses were occupied and everything destroyed. Mme. Sourice had three sons killed. Mme. Gesnier lost her only child, a son (her husband already dead). It's not that they are morbid or sad anymore; it's that I have never encountered this before and nothing is free from it. Also the people's acceptance (it has been over twenty years) is puzzling, or at least it doesn't make it easier for me to take in.

Again, Margot Lafontaine—I have not met her. She is sixty, a nurse, and lives in Paris. Her house is very lovely but rather small for eleven people. It is an old farmhouse, quite modest originally, and is being fixed up in a rustic manner quite slowly or . . . from year to year. It has six rooms, two of which we don't use as bedrooms (the dining-sitting room and the kitchen). All the rooms are small for a large family. Anyway there is electricity. The running water cannot be used for drinking, just washing etc. There is a spring nearby. No hot water—has to be heated on gas burners.

We spent four nights there. Everyone but us has had a bit of turista *but all are fine now.*

Mama's house needs a lot of work. [We were putting ceilings into at least half the rooms.] *The kitchen, which was never civilized—being just for servants to work in and on the bottom floor, with dumbwaiters etc. . . . . anyway it was a farmhouse with low ceilings and all, but a gentleman farmer—not like Margot Lafontaine's place—it is quite large with huge rooms, and done by the Friesekes in an elegant manner. This looks a little sad and silly in the form of wallpaper hanging in strips from the wall, of cupids of course, and a lid here and there of dear china. The terraced garden is very rich with cows and sheep.*

Nick and I are now in our bedroom (Mama's room when she was a little girl). By firelight, candlelight and gas lantern light it looks fine, but . . . tomorrow as the sun rises I will once again see the dirt and feel the dirt. It is late. Somehow none of this is what it is like here—it is more of an outline.

In the same mail (demonstrating that their daughter had married an incorrigible optimist who showed more promise in advertising than he did in real estate), I had put my own letter to Julia's parents:

July 22, 1968

This is a lovely country; it rains all day and the sun shines all day and geese walk up and down the lawn [sic]. *Christopher wears his birthday raincoat all the time, as well as some French boots we got him. Someone goes shopping every day. There is so much needed for the house, as well as for the survival of its customers. Since there is as yet no electricity (they are putting it in now and then, when reminded) we have no fridge; so shopping has to be done almost this morning for this evening. But we are in process of arranging for gas stove, hot water,* chauffage central; *we've got glass in the windows; and we've painted the kitchen; the toilets work when you pour water into them, which we get from the pump out back. We've got beds. We are moving right along.*

The last roll of film, if it comes out, should give you a good idea of the outside of the house and the grounds. The little peasant-looking houses are on either side of the main house and are both inhabited. The road, or lane, goes down to the main road by means of a steep hill and there is a fairly constant stream of animal traffic: goats, chickens, sheep, cows, ducks, turkeys. . . . The ruins of the cider press are halfway down the hill in front of the house, as you look over the valley; the ruins of the stable to the left.

You can still guess at what the house was once. Some of the fur-

niture is left, a couple of the rugs terribly battered. No paintings, of course. We can't think in terms of restoring it. It would be difficult and the result would be most uncomfortable without a slew of servants. What is making me most impatient right now is the wait for the stuff I've ordered so that I can put up bookshelves, so that we can get all the books out of closets, cupboards and attic, and look into them.

We're off this morning to Honfleur, or Caen, or a castle to look at Delacroix paintings and a moat—depending on the weather in half an hour.

Now. The room in which I am sitting is the world's perfect guest room. . . .

"There were eight in Tante Margot's generation that Julia could tell you of," I said to Margaret and Ruth. "One male, who got the house, and seven females, including Suzette and Charlotte's mother, who lived the next town over, and Thérèse's mother. The Lafontaines' house"—I pointed to it; we'd been walking along the road, uphill, in the direction of the town, between steeply rising fields bordered with fern, thistles, nettles, or horsetail, under the dripping trees that lined the road, Andalouse always keeping to the middle, as indifferent to the rain as if it were mere chickens—"there, on the left, the funny-looking brick one with the steep roof and the hundred chimneys and enough windows to qualify as a château—we thought of it as Victorian, but it's really late sixteenth-century and has a tennis court somewhere. It gets called either La Maison Mère or Le Château Lafontaine."

"It's younger than yours," Ruth said.

"Depending on whom you believe," I warned. "But it was built to be splendid, unlike ours, which had its splendor thrust upon it."

TWENTY-EIGHT

We continued uphill, our rubber boots clunking on the pavement or squelching in the mud beside it, and crossed the spring from which we had drawn our drinking water that first summer, in three-foot-tall plastic pitchers that we hauled back to Tante Margot's *chaumière*. Off to our right, from a vantage point in the road high enough that we could see straight across the valley as far as my house, the swirl of caked mud in a drive showed the industry of the Bouquerels' farm. Year-round residents of the town, they did dairy, the whole business, as it used to be done on my land—or rather, the land that I realized I was accidentally thinking of as mine. We drank in the scents of dairy, and grass, and earth, and rain, with woodsmoke wreathing through it.

"There's your house," Margaret said, rubbing it in. She pointed back at the black cube shining in the rain; Ben's smoke wiggled upward from the chimney on the far end from us, crows wheeling around it as if it carried something edible. "It just takes your heart and gives it a good jerk, doesn't it?"

I nodded.

"And from here, the prospect pleases. It looks perfect from this spot," Margaret said. "There's nothing like it in Cambridge. Not even in Brooklyn."

We went past the café, which in the twenties had been a one-room grocery store in a house the rest of which was lived in, as was still the case. Outside the café, on the small flagstone terrace across from the church, stood a few plastic tables and chairs of the type that collects half a cup of rainwater in the seat. Striped umbrellas spread open above the tables dripped rain. Within the café's open doorway, two men in blue were improving the morning with a smoke and a drink, and talking with madame at the bar.

The church of Notre Dame, where our first three children had made their First Communions (though none of them more than once), sat in its churchyard in a Y of roads. Other than this and the café, there was not much commercial (or institutional) activity left in Mesnil, really. The string of small residences that had once held shops were now only residences. Out of sight from where we stood, the new school built after the war functioned only occasionally, as a *salle des fêtes* (festival hall). I told Margaret and Ruth how I had spent the longest afternoon of my life there the summer Julia and I swore to take advantage of every cultural occasion offered (free).

Someone discovered there was to be a Grand Festival de la Musique on a Sunday afternoon and off we went, taking whatever guest was with us at the time, and whatever children we had. We packed into the very middle of the room, which was filled with many strangers as well as everyone in the town, including old M. Lafontaine and Mme., who had long since celebrated their *noces d'or* (golden wedding anniversary). The chairs were small and hard, and the first half of the concert turned out to be accordion music played by children scrubbed and dragged in from far and wide. Each child, and each child's selection, was introduced by a smooth professional emcee in a tuxedo. Although he was only from Lisieux, he could have been an import from Miami, or from outer space, he was so slick. All wore their best, and the occasion had the aura of a major event, almost as important as a First Communion, but one done for TV. Two thirds of the children played "She'll Be Comin' Round the Mountain," which we were already too familiar with in the French milieu, since as part of its lurch into the vernacular in obedience to Pope John XXIII, the church we attended on Sundays had been inflicting on the con-

First Communion of Sadie, 1976. (Left to right, Frances Kilmer, with Christopher, Sadie, and Maizie; Fr. Robert Murray center.)

gregation a sing-along folk Mass in which such popular tunes as "Oh, Susannah" and "Turkey in the Straw" had been subverted to sacred words in French. Even the Sanctus was sung, in French, to the tune of "Tramp, Tramp, Tramp the Boys Are Marching." In our favorite, the Alleluia was substituted for "She'll Be Comin' . . .": our knowledge of the alternate English version got in the way of our piety, and our children gurgled and snorted with rising merriment each time she came around again.

So two thirds of the starched children played "She'll Be Comin' Round the Mountain," and two thirds of them played "Lady of Spain," and each time the selection was announced with a straight face by the emcee with his microphone; and the other two thirds played "Oklahoma!," but very slowly, because "Oklahoma!" was hard on the accordion. Nobody was limited to a single selection, though, so there was a great deal of variety as well—as far as there can be any variety at all, that is, in an accordion concert played by children. I left after the first half, plunging through the crowd during the intermission and skipping the *vin d'honneur*, after learning that in the second half, the same or different children were going to take advantage of the Gounod *portatif* organ, which had been lugged across the graveyard from the church. Julia stayed, with half our party; Julia was always more gregarious than I.

Next to the *salle des fêtes* was the *mairie*, open for one hour every Wednesday, which had notices of local importance tacked to its outside wall, describing hunting season and trash day.

"If the church isn't used, it can't be open," Ruth said, "can it?"

The square eighteenth-century tower with its slate domed cap, which stood at the church's stern, contained a bell that, I told Margaret and Ruth, was connected historically to our house, "or to a former owner of it—whether the Mesnier-Bréards or some-one else, I don't know. But it's a story that should be true, since it came from Monsieur Chevalier."

At that very moment, just as we were crossing the road, Thérèse Chevalier came out of the church carrying a notebook. After the requisite introductions and greetings, which took place in the rain and in the road, she confided to me, "I had to get back to my research." Her car, she said, was parked around back, next to the presbytery. We followed her into the church. The smell of limestone and damp was reminiscent of my downstairs kitchen, with a touch of incense added.

16 août 1968

Yesterday they had Mass at the Mesnil church which is dear [Julia's mother wrote her friend. She had just arrived and was eager to make sense of her surroundings], *with painted wood beams from Viking times of dragons. Land owners of importance were sort of part of it. They are a very old club here. Kenton* [Kilmer, my father] *went to an annual dinner once. Sort of elders, I think.* [Julia's mother was trying to understand Mesnil's chapter of the Frères de Charité.]

After church I met half of the area, most of whom are in one way or another Lafontaines. Mostly I am confused and tomorrow we go to someone's open house. They will remember me but I will not remember them. . . .

"Of course I remember Julia's mother!" Thérèse exclaimed. "She was always having such a good time. How could anyone for-get Mrs. Norris?" And then she was off, eagerly adopting the two new students I had brought her, feeding them what history she could in the brief time allotted.

The inside of the church was rather sad, being so unused.

Thérèse had obtained the key, which was twice the size of the one to my kitchen door, because she had wanted to check a date from one of the marbles inside. The church was small, with a barrel-vaulted roof supported on transverse beams whose gilded and painted ends were carved into dragons' heads. Nobody could say when the heads had been carved, but the gilding, like the paintings copied from Philippe de Champagne's *Nativity* in Rouen, dated from the restoration project of 1874.

"Naturally it's the church that ought to keep the history," Thérèse said. She dragged us halfway up the nave to see the marble tablet on which she had been checking the recorded names and dates of Mesnil's vicars and *curés,* starting with Girard Rosney and Guillaume Harenc, vicars, and Vincent Boissel, *curé,* in 1590. She wasn't sure the tablet was accurate, and planned to cross-check someone's dates. She showed us the place where a plaque commemorated the glorious, brief life of one of the string of lords who had held Mesnil in fief to the Viscount of Auge, thence to the king, in the old days: Messire Ann Houel, *chevalier, seigneur de Morainville et du Mesnil,* killed at twenty-three, in the Battle of Nordlingen in 1645.

While Thérèse talked, Ruth and Margaret looked around at the late stained-glass windows and the sparse collection of commemorative tablets. Mesnil had not been wealthy, not ever.

"As far as records go, at least written ones," Thérèse said, "and we historians always think history is what got written, because that's all we can find—the first record I have from this parish is dated the thirty-first of January 1693, a dispensation of a bann of marriage for Louis Leprevost of Mesnil. You'll still find Leprevosts here. Before that—well, a church stood here in the nine or ten hundreds, but I haven't been able to find anything from that time yet. Church records get lost, too. The first written mention I've found of the town is in the cartulary of the Benedictine monastery across the river, at Saint Hymer, in September of 1410, when Huet le Bonnier, of Fierville, took in fief from the monastery's prior—the prior might as well have been a lord in those days; you can see the revolution coming—a piece of land in Mesnil, for the annual rent of two sous and one capon. That may have been your property, Nick; who knows? It's all there, all the history, if you just look. In 1777, there was Messire Alexandre Duquesne, the curate of Mesnil. In those days the curates were chosen by the local lord, and by 1777 this curate was evidently not up to the task and so resigned his office back to the lord, who lived not in his château in back of the trees there, but in Caen, in the parish of Saint Julian, where he frisked about under a pile of titles—hold on to your hats—*Messire Claude-Jean-Baptiste de Franqueville, chevalier, baron de Morainville, seigneur et patron présentateur du Mesnil, seigneur et patron honoraire de Beuvillers, Livet, le Coullière, Corbon, et autres lieux.*

"After he resigned, Father Duquesne kept half the presbytery that the English people live in now, and a pension of five hundred pounds, as well as some of the presbytery's rental properties in the *commune.* The new curate, Messire le Tetu, moved into the other half of the presbytery and got the rest of the parish rents, of which he had to fork over a portion to the bishop—and the bishop a piece to the pope, and so on. My point is this: this was a lot of hoorah for a parish that never had more than thirty hearths to keep warm. When the revolution hit Mesnil, Le Tetu wouldn't take the constitutional oath but instead hid in England, confiding his furniture to parishioners—the way your grandmother did, Nick, during our war—and not returning until 1803. But what did I want to tell you? Oh, about Duquesne: he was the

TWENTY-NINE

We stood in the vestibule and looked out into the dripping churchyard through the open door. Andalouse padded in and out, exploring in the thick grass, its tips silvered with large drops that gathered size before rolling down further. Above us rose a chorus of votive marble plaques, each a souvenir of thanks or recognition to a saint—most often Sainte Thérèse, the Little Flower, Lisieux's answer to Queen Victoria. Her basilica overlooking the train station in Lisieux far outshone the Crystal Palace.

"I can't put on your father's Algerian hat, or smoke his Gauloise, or make it funny," I apologized, "but I'll do my best. If the church's tower is eighteenth-century, so is the story, because it has to do with the bell—but no, stupid of me, we've got to accommodate a railroad, too, so shift the date to the late eighteen hundreds, after the Mesnier-Bréards.

"Whoever owned or rented my house at the time was a

Freemason, and therefore emphatically anything but Catholic. The parish of Mesnil was in a frenzy of celebration over the anticipated arrival, by train, of the new bell for the church tower—which, coming from Paris, had to be routed through Lisieux. The Bishop of Caen himself had come to join the parishioners, who went down in procession, with a cart and horses and led by the Frères de Charité in their ribbons and *torchères*, to meet the bell at the station at Fierville, unload it, and bring it joyfully back to hoist into place. But our predecessor in the house, with some of his Freemason buddies, sabotaged the plan. They arranged for the train not to stop in Fierville but to steam past the reception parade and pull into Pont l'Evêque, where the bell was unloaded with no ceremony beyond the hoots of a few Freemasons.

"Now you must imagine your father pausing, taking a long drag from his cigarette, and looking at everyone until somebody gave in and said, 'Yes? And then?'

"Well, and then the Freemason who lived in my house died, and his mortal coil was uncoiled and sent to the *pompes funèbres* people in Lisieux to be placed in his casket and readied for burial in Mesnil—in unconsecrated ground, obviously, since he was a Freemason. That meant nothing more than a designated part of the same churchyard that everyone else used; there was only one place a person could be buried in Mesnil, and after all, he had been a neighbor and a citizen. Anyway, the casket was put on the train in Lisieux, and the Freemason's brothers, in their regalia, and with a horse and cart, paraded down to meet it with all due Masonic pomp at the station at Fierville, where they watched the train clatter by without let or hindrance, to dump the casket in the *consigne de bagage*s outside the stationmaster's office in Pont l'Evêque. . . ."

After he died, in September of 1939, my grandfather Frieseke, newly baptized, was buried in a plot chosen for him by the *curé* and located as near as possible to the children on the north side of the church, under the only remaining vestige of the original structure. This Thérèse pointed out to us, a Romanesque arch with a Saxon-looking zigzag of decoration resembling pointed teeth.

"He was a man of such innocence," the *curé* had said. Of the people who now stood in the rain, only Thérèse had known him; I myself had him only through the testimony of his paintings and

Sarah Ann O'Bryan, Paris, ca. 1901.

stories told by others, in which my vivid grandmother tended to predominate.

I knew him and his attractive wife rather well, back when this century was in its swaddling clothes. . . . They were a curious couple in a way, with diametrically opposite characters and, as frequently happens, were devoted to each other. He was slightly introvert, a profound reader, with rather strong opinions which however he generally managed to keep in rein. She was . . . pretty, intelligent, very chic and possessed of a highly developed sense of elfin humor, verging on the diabolic. The following is an illustration of that last quality—an incident which despite their rather retired life [in Paris] *got around and had quite a success at the time.*

On a warm, summery day, she was carrying some parcels and window shopping on the Boulevard des Italiens when she realized she was being trailed by a typical boulevardier of the period—top hat, boutonnière, probably a monocle et al. When she stopped to look in a window he seized the opportunity to exclaim dulcetly how deeply it grieved him to see such an exquisite example of femininity loaded down with parcels. Would she not grant him the great favor of being allowed to carry them for her? She would. With one of her alluring smiles she handed them over—and on they strolled. When they came to the Trois Quartiers she said she had one or two other things to get. Would he mind? On the third floor she bought a large, cheap paper lampshade, had it wrapped up and handed it to him. On the way down she espied a very large sponge which was just the thing Freddy had been looking for, bought it and added it to her cavaliere serviente's *collection. Out in the sunshine again, her gallant said* "Eh maintenant, chère Madame?" "Maintenant, c'est tout, je crois, chez moi, si vous voulez?" "Parfait! *Then if Madame permits, I will call a* fiacre." "Oh, it is such a lovely day and it really isn't far. Don't you think it would be nice to walk?" *So, walk they did, across the Tuileries, across the Seine, up the Rue du Bac and up the entire length of the Boulevard Raspail and finally up the elevator to their apartment. There she pressed the button and when their maid opened the door, shooed her back, turned to her boulevardier with a last, captivating smile, said* "Just a moment, please," *went in, found her husband in his studio in smock and slippers and said,* "Freddy, there is a man out there who brought home some parcels for me. Do give him a good tip."*

*Reminiscence of Morgan Heiskell, quoted in a letter from his son Andrew Heiskell to Norman Hirschl, April 26, 1965.

The Mesnil graveyard was the somber standard French somnolent flock of huge granite or marble sarcophagus-sized tombstones, on many of which were placed the china flowers or "*Regrets éternels . . .*" tablets available in stores everywhere.

I was touched by the presence of a group of these on my grandparents' stone—and simultaneously shocked and chagrined to see how disreputable the monument's cement foundation had become. "*A mon neveu*" ("To my nephew"), read one of the tablets, decorated with plastic pansies. I could not think, for a moment, what uncle or aunt of my grandparents, here in Mesnil . . . impossible. . . .

"It's the children," Thérèse explained. "They move them around at night, for a joke. Children think death has nothing to do with them."

Margaret was looking down at the grave with her own desolation. "I suppose whoever takes on the house gets the grave, too?" she volunteered.

Fresh flowers bloomed at the foot of the Chevaliers' stone, a pot of geraniums that Thérèse herself must have put there. The stone was shipshape, and the gilding legible—in contrast to that above my grandparents, which was now worn away completely. Anyone who wanted to find them would have to know what he or she was doing.

"When it gets too bad, the mayor's office declares the grave abandoned," Thérèse told me. "Then it's assigned to other tenants. That would be sad—a loss for the town."

I took note that I could no longer put off making arrangements with Sanson et Fils, the *pompes funèbres et marbrerie générale* (funeral home and monument maker) in Pont l'Evêque. The state of my grandparents' tomb was a public disgrace, even more shameful than, if similar to, the present condition of their fences.

"The names you see now are often ones you would have found in the sixteen hundreds as well," Thérèse told her audience as we strolled together between monuments. "Leconte, Lecouturier, Leproux, Prévost, Lemercier . . ."

Ruth walked with Andalouse along a cast-iron ornamental enclosure that paralleled the wall between the churchyard and the kitchen garden kept by the English people in back of their presbytery. They already had lettuce coming into head, and Mme. Vera's garden next to the *douet* was not even planted yet. "Is this the unconsecrated ground?" Ruth asked.

"Just the opposite. It's for the people from the château," Thérèse said.

Since it was raining harder now, Thérèse gave us a ride home.

THIRTY

They'd have to lift the stone and start again, the people at Sanson's *pompes funèbres* told me. They'd want to redo the housing of the vault, and replace the rotten cement with black granite, didn't I think, to match the stone? They showed me samples.

I could hear it echoing out of the Old Testament somewhere in Ben's voice, a vatic statement perhaps from the lost Book of Julia: *You have to raise the stone and start again.*

We'd all driven into Pont l'Evêque after lunch, once we had satisfied ourselves that the plumbers had returned. My guests were going to shop in the mostly closed stores (Tuesday, the day after market day, remember?) or look around or collect schedules at the train station or stand gazing from a bridge into the Yvie, or the Calonne, or the Touques, or consider the (closed) public library (once the Hôtel Montpensier), a seventeenth-century solidity in brick and stone with a graceful double entrance staircase, the erstwhile proud home of the Fresnays, whose basement

I happened to know smelled just like mine. I, meanwhile, would make some inquiries concerning repairs to funerary monuments.

The people at Sanson's, being in the sympathy business, were more helpful and reassuring than M. Thouroude in the *quincaillerie.* But as I quickly understood, I was also shopping for something a good deal pricier than a chicken-wire fix to keep owls out of the chimney.

Nothing could be done, I learned, while the ground was wet, but meanwhile they could certainly look and let me have an *estimation.* Monsieur was leaving the country when?

A momentary spasm of rebellion struggled against the inanimate weight of all I was flirting with taking onto my shoulders. I could, if I played my cards right, get out from under it, take the train tomorrow, and have a day or two in Paris before my plane home. I could look at other people's pictures, be cooked for by my friend Madeleine and talk about family, consider the world with Tom, listen to the entertaining fables my godson Gabriel was preparing for me, worry about nothing, wash my clothes— *Merde,* I thought (that much of my French, at least, returning), *I've got all those sheets to deal with.*

"Depending on the weather, and in principle, the day after tomorrow," I said, and gave them my phone number in Mesnil. "Early in the morning."

I found everyone in the cider and calvados store, which, since it was designed expressly for tourism, was obliged to be open. Ben, who knew wine, was bemused by this store's specialization in the Norman *vin du pays.*

"They want you to wait until the calvados is twelve years old," he said, studying a leaflet. Naturally the price increased with the age. The store offered dusty bottles, and dustier bottles, and newer ones that could be put away for future use; and sweet cider called Bréavoine made by the family of a former mayor of Mesnil; and pear cider; and pommeau, a mixture of calvados and cider consumed as an aperitif by persons who did not care that the drink, if not exactly dead, seemed to be living only by galvanic action. There were bottles of something in which the apple was present in its entirety. Growers surrounded the set fruit, at its beginning, with the bottle, which was then tied to the branch while the fruit grew. I liked to think of these trees covered with hanging bottles when the wind blew.

"The calvados we've been drinking from the Intermarché," Teddy said, his Nordic height threatening the top shelves, "the one you've got that rabbit marinating in for tonight—what's wrong with that? It's only two years old. And as for cider, if we're basically talking festered apple juice, what difference . . ."

The assistant, a young man with clean hands and an education, in white shirtsleeves and a tie, who had enough English to take umbrage at Teddy's indifference to his specialization, approached and delivered himself (as if having memorized it in school) of a tract, anointing me as his interpreter: "Believe me, there are growths [*crus*] of cider as different from each other as growths of wine, and the cider of the Vallée d'Auge is especially appreciated. Already in the seventeenth century, were they not remarking a distinction among the 'spicy' [*épicé*], the 'sweet' [*doux*], le Vesque, and le Guillot Roger? Monsieur, you must understand, the kind of apple trees, the nature of the earth, the care applied to the collection of the fruit and to its crushing—all of these have an enormous influence."

He trembled, rose up on his toes, and glowed crimson. Then he gesticulated frantically with both hands, as if he were conducting some independent-minded cygnets in *Swan Lake* who thought this was only a dress rehearsal.

"Doré, tirant légèrement sur le rose, le cidre doit pétiller sans mousser, et surtout être d'une parfaite limpidité" ("Golden, but tending slightly toward rose color, cider should effervesce without foaming, and be above all of a perfect clarity"), he pronounced (or quoted). *"Le digne accompagnement d'un bon repas sera le cidre du pays, justement célèbre"* ("A worthy accompaniment to a good meal will be the region's cider, justly celebrated").*

"In that case, we'll take two bottles of the Bréavoine," Ben said, "if you think it will go with rabbit."

"You could do nothing better for your rabbit. This I swear."

*He may well have been reading, in *Le Pays d'Auge* for November 1955, "La Table en Pays d'Auge," by MM. Patrice Boussel and Georges Poisson.

THIRTY-ONE

On the drive back, my guests persuaded each other that in fairness to the occasion and to the countryside, they ought to do some tourism before they left the next day, though sitting in the house, or marketing, or walking in the rain, or even just watching the strollings of cattle or the activities of birds seemed plenty to justify the term "vacation"—especially if plumbers or Mme. Vera and her rifle added dramatic tension and variety.

They could drive to Bayeux and see the cathedral and Queen Mathilde's tapestry of triumph and desolation (a copy of it decorated my upstairs bathroom, installed as a frieze by Gabriel); or check Pegasus Bridge, liberated on D day by Britain's Fifth Parachute Brigade; or take in any of a dozen castles; or drive about the countryside; or visit Deauville, which wouldn't be cranked up for racing and swimming and the casino life until August, but which still offered a stretch of the long gray Atlantic, shallow and warmed by the Gulf Stream. Or whatever.

In the event that I opted out of their excursion to Honfleur, I could commend to them its wooden church built by ship's carpenters; its active fishing harbor; its museum dedicated to Boudin (the painter, not the sausage—though the variety to be found between one sample and another of either commodity, I warned them . . .). They'd have tea and come back late, they said, unless I needed help with the rabbit.

I didn't have long. I didn't have long to be here, or to think. I'd done nothing but work since I arrived, and none of the work had brought me closer to knowing anything more exact than that I could not bear not to have that work to do. If the decision had been mine, or only mine—but it was not, and in any case, taking over the house was not like a decision, but more like a common-law marriage that a couple of goodwill has backed into, and keeps working on, making thousands of small decisions all the time, if never that big one spoken in the defining moment of "I do." As to the implications . . . "I'll be all right," I told them. "You go ahead."

I saw them off and had tea on my own, in the dining room, where the blossoms on the digitalis were tumbling one by one with wan damp thumps off their tall stems and onto the table—on their way downhill, like everything else. I put beside me a yellow pad on which to start listing the chores that had to be done just to keep the place from sliding further backward; others that would pull it slightly ahead; and still more that were just a matter of housekeeping before I left.

Find wicker tray, I wrote. I hadn't yet been to the guesthouse, M. Braye's. Someone could have taken the tray over there last summer for some reason. I hadn't been to the attic yet, either. One of its window panes, it had seemed to me when I looked up at the house that first night from Mme. Vera's vegetable garden by the stream, did not glare back at sunset as it should, and was probably broken out; but if I confirmed that this was true, it would mean my having to measure the opening, or rather (because nothing was square anywhere in this house, whether door, window, ceiling, or floor), draw the missing pane, and then carry the template into Pont l'Evêque the following day, when the *droguerie* would be open again, to have a new pane cut. And if I was going to do all that, I might as well continue a project for which I had brought down a few picture frames from the attic the previous year, with the idea that I could have mirrors cut for them to brighten up the rooms that needed it. They were still leaning against a bookshelf in the library, next to three quarters of my grandfather's portable landscape easel.

If I went up to the attic to look for the tray—why it would be there I did not need to ask—I'd have to *know* rather than suspect about the window pane.

By the time we returned from town, the plumbers had left, though the afternoon was not over. I saw their tools still in the downstairs kitchen, so I knew they'd gone to get something or were responding to someone else's emergency and would finish here the next day or at some other appropriate time in the future. The latter seemed more likely, since whatever they'd jerry-rigged at least provided me with water, even hot water upstairs in the new shower—which was not, after all, a bad shower. In fact, it was a good shower, and a real improvement. We'd come a long way since 1968. For the time being, it was just worth your life to get into and out of that new shower: a hitch, but one that could be fixed.

The rain stopped and the sun shone in a pure blue sky, slanting in through the dining-room window. It hovered and was greeted by a hoarse barking that I knew to be that of the fox, Mme. Vera's enemy, teasing from the foot of the hill near her gar-

Frieseke's painting of the building, now Mme. Vera's, in which he kept his studio. Oil on canvas, 20 × 24 inches, ca. 1924. Collection Montclair, New Jersey, Museum of Art.

den; the bark sounded curiously like her own bark of rage that morning when she missed him, failing in her quest to nail him on the door of the garage. The slates of the *auvent* under my window began to steam as vigorously as my cup of tea, and then the rain started again.

At six o'clock I was still looking at my yellow pad. It was all too much to keep track of. After the entry *Find wicker tray*, my invention had quailed at the number of things a person could and should do every day if any of this were to make sense. It all seemed stupid and impossible, but nothing could correct my basic condition of hopeless affection: not to take on the house was simply to lose it forever. "First raise the stone" was as useful a nugget of platitudinous advice to me as it would have been to Lazarus once he was underground; in my present mood, it seemed as taunting an injunction as *Find wicker tray*. Obviously, like Lazarus, I needed help.

I was arranging my rabbit in a roasting pan in the downstairs kitchen when I heard M. Joffroy's car. I had the upper half of the Dutch door to the driveway open to give me light. The rain had slowed to a clear drizzle. The butcher had tied the rabbit and wrapped it in a caul, so that it looked less like a specific beast, though its legs still emerged, bound in against the body. I wouldn't start cooking it until my guests returned; while it was in the stove, I'd have time enough to trim the green beans and do the rest of it.

M. Joffroy pried himself out of his car and called into the kitchen, *"Voici le maçon!"*—as pleased to have landed a mason so quickly as he had been to discover the snails breeding on my wall.

Normans are either tall and fair or short and dark, and the mason, M. Toffolon, was as emphatically of the latter persuasion as M. Joffroy was of the former. A square man on the mature side of fifty, he brushed his hands on his dusty white canvas pants, and we all shook.

"Belle maison," M. Toffolon growled, looking up at the streaming expanse of slate wall before I led them inside. *"Mais on dit qu'elle travaille un peu"* ("Lovely house, but they say she's working"—or moving—"a bit"). He spoke affectionately, as one would of a beloved elderly aunt heading into her thirteenth marriage.

"It's the floor of the *salle d'eau*," M. Joffroy said. "Two flights up. Be careful; all day I have been having nightmares about it."

Again he did his imitation of Rodin's *Thinker* plunging three stories into the hearty soup of the *enfer*.

The two men sniffed my rabbit marinade appreciatively—calvados, garlic, mace, and tarragon were hard to pass by without comment—and M. Joffroy gave me the high compliment of repeating the gesture he had used that morning when thinking of *escargots de Bourgogne* presented on the table.

I put my rabbit in the fridge to protect it from flies and covered it to keep it from drying out, and we went upstairs. Monsieurs Joffroy and Toffolon had to stand in the dining room waiting while I arranged extension cords and lamps to get some light into the jam closet. I wanted first to show them the problem from below.

"*Belle maison,*" M. Toffolon repeated. "What is its date?"

I had to confess I did not know, adding that my mother claimed to have seen the date 1493 under the cement outside, to the left of the step into the library.

"*Ça se peut,*" M. Toffolon said, shrugging. "It may have been a convent, with all the dormers it has in the attic—they used to do that so the nuns could sleep up there."

I noticed him surreptitiously shifting his weight on the dining room's tiles, testing for loose ones. "A house like this," he said, "she's always getting into some kind of trouble or another, isn't she? But it will take her a long, long time to fall down completely."

That must be a common concept in Europe, I thought, *since Teddy used very similar words.*

M. Toffolon followed me across the vestibule at the foot of the grand staircase, and I pointed up at the worrying bathroom floor.

"Ooh, trouble," M. Toffolon said, looking down and motioning us back.

"No, it's up there," M. Joffroy and I told him, both of us pointing upward together.

M. Toffolon bounced delicately on his broad boots and stared down at the floor, shaking his head. "Let's go downstairs," he insisted.

THIRTY-TWO

At the bottom of the cellar steps, three feet from the wastepipe from the upstairs toilet, in the laundry room where cheeses had once been made and where the next day I would determine, after my guests had gone, whether or not the washing machine still functioned (that is, if the plumbers were finished with their work by then), the three of us stood together like—to continue the metaphor from Rodin's canon of sculpture—the burghers of Calais about to step out of the besieged town to greet their English conquerors.

M. Toffolon was feeling better. "There, I knew it," he said, pointing up at the beam that was supposed to be supporting that side of the grand staircase as well as the jam-closet floor and everything above it. The end of the beam was resting on a curled piece of lead pipe that the plumber's *gars* had not got to yet. "I could feel the floor was soft [*molle*]," M. Toffolon said. "As you see, the end of the beam is rotted away."

He took a *tournevis* (screwdriver—I knew the word now, after spending a hard few minutes years before trying to act one out for M. Thouroude, having once again left my dictionary behind at the house) from his pocket and scrabbled at the softened end of oak, which was attempting to slide the rest of the way down the inside of the wall.

"Here's your problem," he reassured me.

It now seemed to me that instead of just the upstairs-bathroom floor, the entire house was collapsing, and my face must have expressed that hideous conclusion.

"*Ce n'est pas grave,*" my fellow burghers kept assuring me, admiring the fit of the noose around my neck. "Half of the beams in the house rested on the walls when it was made, and this one even in the dirt of the garden. Over time, as the ends rot—and oak takes a long time to rot, that's why they used it to make ships—you can build up new supports inside the rooms, and *voilà!* she is in business once again," explained the mason.

"All we have to do," M. Toffolon continued, "before we get to the bathroom floor, is raise this beam to where it was and then support it with a new *poteau*—"

"Of oak," M. Joffroy interrupted.

"But of course, always of oak." Mr. Toffolon spread his arms in the gesture used by those conveying unlikely innocence or reassurance. "You will have nothing to worry about, Monsieur. Always oak, a beautiful oak post we will place here." He dusted his hands before patting the stone wall under the errant beam as if it were the flank of that same game but aging aunt he had complimented earlier. "Now we will look upstairs. The plumbers are working here?" He shook his head, climbing in front of me. "As I have often said, water is the mortal enemy of architecture. When you have pipes, you have a river running through your house. Naturally there is trouble. It is like keeping goats in your garden: nobody would do that."

Before he left, M. Toffolon stood in the drive looking up at M. Braye's house, which was surrounded by cattle. It was all on one floor, thirty feet long and ten wide, with a peaked roof covered in newish slate. Since we had put the dormers in ourselves, there was nothing to indicate that it had ever been inhabited by anyone more nunnish than my Great-aunt Janet.

"That's your *old* house," he said. "You can see it's where they would have built—there's a spring right above it, see? that little flat plateau with nettles on it (they like water, nettles), that's its housing. There's water in there, a *source.* I don't even have to go up the hill to look. For people who kept sheep or cows, maybe while Charlemagne was king—who knows?—it would have been ideal. The way people built didn't change until they began using steel, which I won't touch."

He showed us how the cottage had grown, one segment at a time, laterally, starting from a thick stone cube about six feet by six (the room I'd made into the kitchen), which he was sure had been the first building on the property—a one-room house with rubble walls, to serve a family of whatever size it had to. "People were poor in those days," he said. "Whenever 'those days' were."

They climbed together into M. Joffroy's car, M. Toffolon having promised to consider the situation and give me an *estimation,* as well as an idea of whether the work could be done before the August renters arrived. I tried to be jovial, but I was upset, not only because he had discovered so much more wrong than I had expected but also because it was so easy to see. I should have seen it, and the plumbers should have seen it—but I especially, given that I went up and down the basement stairs ten times a day at least.

It was small consolation to know that one of two things had happened: either the beam had rotted due to ground moisture absorbed over the centuries, and in subsiding had inflicted the large, familiar crack in the right wall of the grand *escalier* and caused the bathroom floor to sag, thus distressing the joints in the pipes serving the toilet, which eventually sprang a leak that rotted the floor; or, conversely, the toilet's leaking had rotted the floor, and the water's downward progress along the wall had slowly destroyed that end of the main beam, leading it to slip its position. . . .

However it had begun, it sounded like an awful lot of carpentry to me, and a big chunk of money. I watched M. Joffroy attempt to turn his car in the narrow driveway halfway down the hill—and at once back into, break, and then get stuck on what was left of one of the remaining cement fence posts. I went to help them dislodge from the shards without the loss of their gas tank or oil pan, and, joking with graveyard humor, exclaimed, "And now look, you've destroyed my beautiful fence!"

"No problem," M. Joffroy said, giving M. Toffolon a good nudge. "*Il est maçon*" ("He's a mason"). "He is an expert in cement."

They drove away, laughing.

I was just pulling on my boots so I could go up the pasture to M. Braye's and have a look around when I heard a car in the drive and thought it meant it was time to put the rabbit in. But it wasn't my guests, nor any car I knew. Someone for Mme. Vera, I concluded, and I opened the gate that kept cattle out of the space immediately around the house (though only so long as they consented to use a gate, and only when I was in residence).

The car sputtered to a halt, and a charming young woman got out—robust and graceful, red-cheeked, with her hair in a close red curl, and wearing a pink raincoat, I noticed as she came around the car.

"Monsieur Quilmère?" she asked. She spoke the name as if she had worked hard to get the pronunciation close to the one I use.

I admitted it.

"They told me at Sanson's that you had come."

"For a few days," I said. I realized I was being slow to show common courtesy, and shook the hand she held out.

"You are with Sanson's?" I asked. It had taken me a moment first to recall what Sanson's was (the *pompes funèbres et marbrerie générale*) and then to imagine that this wholesome and happy-looking person could be fresh from standing in a rainy graveyard calculating the cost of repairs to my grandparents' grave. She must be arriving with Sanson's *estimation.*

"Will you come inside?" I asked her, noticing the drops of drizzle beginning to accumulate in her hair. "You've been very quick."

She followed me into the kitchen, looking puzzled. "No," she said. She looked at the rabbit I had taken out when I heard the car coming up the driveway. "It smells very good. You should put on plenty of black pepper. You are yourself the cook?" I nodded. "And make sure the oven is very hot before you put it inside, so the outer integument will receive a shock. Then the flavor will stay inside."

"Thank you," I said. So far this apparition seemed as strange, as unheralded, as perfect, and as likely to be a myth, or *obs.* and *poet.*, as had my morning's nightingale.

"I am Mme. Turquétil," she said, and then waited. We already knew that I was M. Quilmère. "And no, I am not with Sanson's, but we have known each other, Mme. Sanson and I—young

Mme. Sanson—since school, and she told me you had arrived." She waited for me to say something. I had always objected to that lazy and ubiquitous line used to bring new characters onto the TV screen—"What are you doing here?"—and I started trying to think of alternatives that would achieve the same result.

"My name was not Turquétil before," my visitor volunteered. "It was Perrossier. Yvette."

"Ah," I said.

"I married Hervé Turquétil last October," she said. She smiled and blushed and looked still more charming.

I thought, *And so her garter is even now fluttering from the aerial of Hervé Turquétil's car.*

Because I was the third generation of my family in Mesnil, and there were still godchildren or children of old friends of my mother's or grandparents' in the neighborhood, I now began to fear, as I often did, that I knew this person but had simply (and completely) forgotten her—and I had been so frank in greeting her at the beginning that I could not now easily say, *Who are you? Why are you here?* If Julia had been with me, she would have remembered Yvette Perrossier, and known how she was related to the Lafontaine family—or whether it was in fact Hervé Turquétil who was the link to that great chain of being.

"And Madame O'Banyon, she is well?" Madame Turquétil, née Perrossier, asked.

A small light gleamed at the end of the tunnel. If the connection was to the previous summer's renters, then perhaps I could be forgiven for not knowing this person. I replied that Madame O'Banyon had been well the last I'd heard, and that all her family was also well, but they would not be coming back this year. Mme. Perrossier and I began to get along quite well, though I still had no idea why she was here. At last she said with regret that she must be going since Hervé expected his dinner. She smiled at me proudly and went back to her car as I turned to my rabbit. When she appeared in the doorway again, she was holding, balanced against a cocked and comely hip, my wicker tray, piled high with folded laundry.

"I did these for Madame O'Banyon after she left," said Mme. Turquétil (Turketil was the name of one of the pirate Rollo's foremost henchmen) as she put my no-longer-missing sheets and towels on the kitchen table next to the rabbit, on my no-longer-missing tray.

"Let me pay you," I said quickly. I was so pleased to have my tray back that I would have been a soft touch for anyone.

"No, no," she said. Mrs. O'Banyon had paid her in advance; all that was taken care of. Fortunately Sanson's had told her I was back, since she had not wanted to come into the house when it was empty to deliver the clean laundry.

She pulled my missing key from her coat pocket and put it in my hand, then waited while I shifted it to the other hand so I could shake hers good-bye—though at that moment I would have gladly kissed it instead, not to mention the entire rest of her, so clumsily pleased was I at having everything restored to the way it should be.

You have been too long away from your loving wife, I said to myself in the tone of voice that mature men far from home hate to hear when they are idly thinking of covering strange young Frenchwomen with kisses.

THIRTY-THREE

The car taking Margaret, Ben, Teddy, Ruth, and Andalouse down my driveway the next morning, and then northward toward Amsterdam, dragged the rain away with it as if it were attached to its rear end with a tow chain, leaving the early morning steaming under a sun that seemed as flagrant, bright, and dependable as any eighth-grade girl. Although I felt I'd barely arrived, it was already time for me to start closing the house—but not in the drastic, final way that prepared it for the storms and solitude of winter, because it was to be lived in throughout August, and there would be masons and (I had to hope) plumbers here in the meantime.

I put in the first load of sheets, wondering at the native frame of mind that let me feel both exultant and justified because sunshine would allow me to hang out two loads of laundry. Why had I not pursued the acquaintance of Mme. Turquétil? Because I liked the work, which emphasized the dependence of the house on me.

This solitary place resisted solitude. My brief time had filled the fridge with more than I could eat or drink now that I was alone again; I'd give the overflow to Mme. Vera when I left. Ben had, of course, found things to buy in Honfleur while they were touring, and they had returned with the satisfied anticipation of the seduced.

"We just brought samples," Ben and Margaret promised, as they led the way into the kitchen with plastic bags. "To have while the rabbit cooks, you know. The people in the stores were very helpful."

They pulled out a bottle of Ricard, the clear liquor that turns cloudy with water and is a replacement for Pernod, tasting of liquorice; and a Sancerre to have with the rabbit if the cider

*The dining room, 1988. (*Left to right, *Beth Chapin, Kenton Kilmer, the author, Julia, Moira Chapin, Thomas, Gillian, Dana Perrone, Jacob Kilmer, Jen and Lachlan Youngs, Craig Adams, Maizie Kilmer.) Photo Walter Chapin*

proved insufficient; and otherwise, Ben said, "We can try this Bordeaux—two bottles just in case. You can always use it." *Pâtés* made from game, or salmon, or dreams, or the livers of geese; celeriac and pickled eggplants; stuffed eggs, quails in aspic, and herring eating themselves from the tail end; cooked artichokes; fresh peaches; seven or eight cheeses and an assortment of breads, as well as the tarts that always (like children dressed for an accordion concert) are better only to look at. It made for a gay and colorful spread, everything scattered across the tablecloth under the weeping foxgloves.

While we assaulted the aperitifs, Ruth made salad and Teddy did battle with green beans that were so thin and tender and stringless they would have cooked in response to the mere threat of heat. The free range of the guests made up for a certain lack of imagination in their sedentary host, who hadn't been able to get much further than meat and potatoes after all (though the meat *was* rabbit).

"What were those pesky birds carrying on this morning in the rain?" Margaret asked while I was dismembering the roasted rabbit. "That's what we should be eating. Serve them right, birds that won't let you sleep." By now it was quite late; we'd been taking our time, all of us, including the rabbit.

I had forgotten the predawn nightingales, whose presence Margaret was substantiating. Teddy had not heard them, nor had Ben or Ruth.

The thing is not to start again, exactly, I thought, *but to be in a new context, where what you expect to do or be is influenced by a naïveté born of insurmountable ignorance. You have to learn it all with your senses, like a two-year-old—like Christopher years ago pulling the snails off his great-grandparents' tombstone and trying to eat them.*

It would not be a bad place to have my grandchildren visit, if that should develop, I thought.

Meanwhile, all I need to do is learn to hear that racket of bird-song, know it's a nuisance, and be prepared to eat the creatures that make it. And I might as well cook them using a French recipe. Therefore (to adapt a suitable recipe from Dumas):

> Pluck, but do not eviscerate, your nightingales; then singe, truss, and cover with slices of bacon and buttered paper, and roast. Into a pot put a little gravy and *coulis*, one glass of white wine. Bring to a boil. Add the juice of one lemon and twelve juniper berries previously blanched. When your nightingales are done, take off the paper and bacon, simmer in the *coulis*, arrange on the platter, skim the fat from the sauce, and serve hot.

"Your nemesis was nightingales," I told Margaret.

"Nightingales or not, they woke me," Margaret said. "I don't carry on like that when *I* get up at night. But I shall tell everyone in Brooklyn that I heard the singing of the nightingales and was elevated with enchantment to a state bordering upon hyperbole."

Closing the house after they left meant struggling against sentiment, because it always felt as though it might be the last time. And if our decision was not to take this on . . .

By ten o'clock I had one load of sheets hung out and the second load grinding, and the upstairs rooms looked over. The house had its own inertia, I realized, considering it now that I was alone again; and more so since it was an old house. When it had been empty, it took some time for it to become acclimatized to human inhabitants; but once it had been inhabited awhile, it would relinquish the human spirit only with reluctance. It was not so many years before that my daughter Sadie, who always championed the cause of the afflicted, had sung lullabies to spiders in the billiard room; and not so long before *that* (though it was long before *I* knew her) that her great-grandmother, also Sadie, and herself the daughter of another Sadie, had listened to the racket of the nightingales while lying in the same room, her cheek branded by the monogram of her wedding sheet.

The sun shone as if it had never heard of rain. I had no need to go to town today, or to step off the property at all. I could catch an evening train to Paris, or go in the morning, or perhaps—I had a whole day with no obligations, and all that new canvas I had brought: why not start making my own mess?

At three-thirty, painting on the first terrace of the garden, I heard the phone and reached it in time to get M. Joffroy's message, interpreting M. Toffolon's *estimation:* almost as accurate as if he had read my mind. It was not as bad as I had feared, but then again it was as much as I could stretch to spare. There was no question that it had to be done, but nonetheless I told M. Joffroy that I must think about it and call him back; meanwhile, could he thank M. Toffolon for his speedy attention, and for his promise to have the work done before the summer tenants came?

At four-forty-five I was working on the second terrace of the garden. The light was moving fast; the hawks were working overhead, the rainwater working, fresh out of the sky, in the cement pond, the waterbugs working on its surface, the doves working in the eaves of the house around the other side, the chickens working in the dirt—and Mme. Vera was sprawled on her back in the sun of her courtyard, catching the rays, the sunlight glancing off the flowered print of her pink dress. I could see her from my van-

The author gardening, 1986. Photo Bette Noble

tage point in the deep grass that had once been my grandmother's cutting garden, overlooking the First Communion party.
I could hear the rattle of the young goats on the steaming corrugated iron above the cider press, which I began to imagine I
could roof instead with corrugated translucent plastic and use as
a studio, though there would be no way to heat it and nothing to
see from inside it unless windows were put in. The phone rang
and took me inside again, wiping the paint off my hands.

Mme. Sanson the elder told me that M. Sanson was just now
returned from Mesnil, having looked at my grave, and had left in
my mailbox at the foot of the driveway a catalog illustrating my
options, which she would now describe to me. I could let them
know what I had decided in due course. If I understood her suggestions correctly, it appeared that the minimum response to the

situation in the churchyard would be an investment almost exactly equivalent to the mason's estimate—again, the limit of what I could make available right now.

I thanked Mme. Sanson and told her I would let them know.

At twenty of six I was working in the garden, still on the second terrace, feeling pleased at the colors inventing themselves in the water of the pond, when the telephone rang and called me back inside, this time to a male voice, American.

"Bob Rafferty here. Florence O'Banyon told me if we were ever in the area—she loved it so very much—and we happened, my wife and I, Harriet—we were in Normandy, revisiting the beaches, and I thought, well, as a friend of Florence O'Banyon, she'd never forgive us if we didn't telephone, in case there was someone home."

I was barely at home, but I could hardly deny being here at this point. I made a little conversation, while keeping a weather eye on how the light was moving, as I talked, on the far side of the dining-room door, making everything furious, and wild, and peaceful. Bob Rafferty explained that he'd been one of the bomber pilots deployed to soften up the Normandy defenses prior to D day; having recently married for a second time, he was now touring the country with his new wife, to show her where he'd been. And since Florence O'Banyon had told him if he was in the area . . .

"Where are you?" I asked.

"By a curious coincidence, it turns out we're in Mesnil. I'm calling from the café."

Not in recorded history (at least not since 1410) has anyone ever been in Mesnil by a coincidence, curious or otherwise. I told him how to find the place, instructed him to close the gate behind his car so the cows would not escape (a sacrifice I was not yet prepared to make to the spirit of the place, though it did occur to me from time to time), and advised him to be careful on the driveway. Then I went back to work for the ten minutes left me before they arrived.

THIRTY-FOUR

The Raffertys refused all offers of tea or nourishment. They were staying in Paris, had just come out for the day, and were due back in Paris for dinner. But Florence O'Banyon had told them so much about how wonderful her stay here was. Would I mind very much letting them see the house?

When Bob Rafferty cracked his head on the lintel going into the salon, because I forgot to warn him, he winked and said, "Oh, yeah, Florence told me you have to do that thirteen times before you remember." Florence had been so enthusiastic about all the things you could do, they told me: swimming at Deauville, going to the races and the casino; shopping; playing tennis at a court you could reserve nearby; going horseback riding; or just getting in the car and driving, then spending hours cooking in that wonderful Old World kitchen.

Wonderful Old World kitchen? I thought. The glamorous O'Banyon life sounded nothing like ours here. We tended more to paint, move books, make curtains, or carry accumulated odd things out to the pasture to burn.

My visitors exclaimed over the toilets with the tanks up against the ceiling, with their pull chains and the china handles that said *tirez* on them. They loved the catwalk across the Old World bathroom floor; in fact, Harriet Rafferty's word for it was "Perfect." Everything about the house was so familiar to me by now that nothing seemed exotic, quixotic, strange, or even particularly troublesome anymore. By the end of dinner the night before, I had been easily back into the routine of cooking simultaneously in two kitchens on two floors, even as I listened for the splintering, muddy crash of a guest's appearing suddenly through the ceiling of the dining room. I'd got the sheets dry and off the line and folded and put back into the billiard room. I knew exactly where I was. Bob Rafferty cracked his head on the lintel coming out of the salon and said, "Eleven more times and I'll have it."

He and his wife were of about the same age; he must have been quite a young pilot. He was lean and tall and dressed in resort clothes, while his wife, equally lean but small, was in jeans and a sweatshirt, but otherwise they were well matched in temperament.

"I thought, since we were going to be on a farm," she said. "I mean, since we *might* be . . ."

And so I gave them an abbreviated tour of the outside as well, as Bob Rafferty told me something of what the D-day action had been like, at least as much of it as he had seen. "And this house," Harriet Rafferty interjected, "it must have suffered terribly during the war, what with the Germans."

"Not so much the Germans, but the refugees," I said.

"But then you, your name—that's German, isn't it?" Mrs.

Rafferty pointed out. In truth, I'd never thought so, since my father's people had been in the United States long enough to lose their ethnic identity, and my father's father, well before he left for the front, had abdicated the lapsed German ancestry in favor of a usurped Irish one, announcing, "I'm half Irish and no mathematician." My mother's father's people had spoken German back in Michigan, yes. But we'd never been anything but plain Americans.

"Amazing," Bob Rafferty said. "Isn't it always the way? It's the French people who did the damage in their own country, whereas the Germans, who were supposed to be the enemy . . ."

I pointed out that the Germans hadn't had any reason to trash the place, believing it would remain theirs by right of conquest, whereas the refugees had been cold and had had very little of anything, including hope. It was the difference between rich and poor. The simplicity of this contrast had not occurred to any of us before, and we looked at it together for a little while before the Raffertys left for dinner in Fontainebleau. I rode down the drive with them to help them get through the cows and deal with the gate, and to retrieve the Sanson brochure from the mailbox.

Walking back up the drive, I realized I'd forgotten lunch. When I got to it, I could have a hell of a final dinner of leftovers. I'd close the shutters and catch the earliest train for Paris in the morning and have a whole day to be a tourist before traveling home light, carrying nothing but my overnight bag.

At eight twenty-seven, with hours of daylight left, I was painting on the second terrace when the telephone rang.

THIRTY-FIVE

Is it beautiful?" Julia asked. Her voice had in it the hope and fear that accompany a loved one who is insured for air travel but heading home.

"I'm just leaving," I said, miffed at how long she'd taken to respond to her cue.

"Tell me."

"I've got the upstairs closed and swept, and—"

"I mean tell me it's beautiful, stupid," Julia said. "It's almost too late, because you're coming home and then I'll have to hate all of that mess that follows you everywhere."

"As soon as Margaret and Ben left, it stopped raining," I said. "Those ribbons of wild blue sky—"

"No, make it rain," Julia interrupted. "I miss you and I miss the rain. All those troubles of life. Make it rain and give it to me. You're there all alone and I'm here all alone, so tell me. Make it rain. Start again. And don't forget that the phone costs money. I ask you, is it beautiful?"

I looked across the brilliance of the valley and started lying to my wife.

"It's a light rain, so slow you don't know it's there until you realize that the steady *plock* you've been hearing for the last hour is the drip onto the *auvent* from the leak in the gutter above the upstairs-kitchen window. The cows are standing facing toward the foot of the driveway, about twenty, thirty feet across the fence, up to their knees in nettles. They look as if they hear something coming, but nothing is coming: everything that was going to come today has already come and gone. But that doesn't stop them from calling to whatever it is, giving their opinion. The rain doesn't stop the doves. They're worse than that old washing machine we had. Everything out the window is green with gray stripes, diagonal, on account of the direction of the rain. There's no wind. The rain just leans one way to get a rest from leaning the other way, which is what it was doing before."

"And so the air is cold and sort of thick—like wet sheets?" Julia said. "But billowing with wind that they feel, even if you can't."

"You mean if the sheets are caught short on the line. Speaking of sheets—"

"Maybe you'd better keep sheets out of this," Julia warned.

"What have you been doing?" I asked her.

"You have a garden here," Julia said. "A perfectly good one, with the extra added attraction that it comes with me. Never mind. Go on, we were looking down the hill through the orchard."

"The pear trees are in flower, only a few of them here and there. Their white blossoms spring back each time the load of water gets to be more than they want. The apple trees are just in leaf now. The rain, gathered into drops big enough to fall, makes

Julia, the Grim Reaper, 1988. Photo Harriet Griesinger

a clicking in their leaves. Their trunks are darker where the water runs down them. I have a red car that the rain is rolling down, onto the driveway, which is all grass and that plant you claim is chamomile, but which Thérèse, who sends you her regards, says is something else that I made her write down, but now I've lost the piece of paper. It's been raining for days."

"You go to Normandy on purpose and then complain about the rain?"

"You're the one who wanted rain," I said. "I'm just trying to oblige."

" 'Trying to oblige,' he says, standing on the other side of the Atlantic Ocean and spending all our money on the telephone. How about you oblige me when you're home? I need a hole for my new rose that's trying to flower. I'm mud up to the gills."

"You're working in the garden?"

I heard her take a gulp. She'd come inside from the garden and decided to call me while she was having tea. "Go on," she said. "It's raining?"

I felt I was running down. "Maybe in Germany at night all cows are gray," I tried, "but here I saw one last night strolling after dark—midnight it was, and raining—and it looked like a white map of the world moving along the pasture snorting and chewing, a warm, hairy universe minding its own business out there."

"Not like that," Julia said. (*Haven't you learned anything?*) "Listen, we got caught in a downpour, you and I, walking below the house, so we ran and got under the chestnuts in the driveway, where it's always wet but the thick leaves keep the rain from falling on us, until we say the hell with it, it's never going to stop, and we cut down the mud bank to the *douet*."

I interrupted with some news. "There are no fish this year. Thérèse says it's because Monsieur Terbiault dumped the entire contents of his stable into it upstream in February, and everything turned green, including the fish, which floated and swelled. We missed a big stink, she said. But now it's clear brown water with wild geraniums drooping toward it, and cress growing, which I had always heard proves there's no pollution; maybe it doesn't mind what comes out of a barn."

I heard Julia's fingers tapping with impatience. This was a crucial time, and I was getting it all wrong. "Okay, we're standing in the flat stretch you like, with our boots sucking mud, and a motorbike splutters along the road toward Fierville with a fat lady on it. I can't tell who it is, she's so bundled up. The road's all purple from the rain, and from here you can't see the goddamned house, which needs several thousand dollars' worth of structural work I wasn't expecting, or the graveyard, which also needs—"

"I thought you were telling me how beautiful it was," Julia said. "You go all the way to France and forget how to seduce your wife?"

"Sorry."

"What are we wearing?" Julia prompted.

"You can have that old brown raincoat of my mother's, since you never pack a raincoat because you like to travel light. We're exactly alike. I've got my red coat that's too short, so I'm wet from my waist to my boot tops, but not for long since there's no place for all that water to go but down, into the boots. You won't wear anything on your head, because you are that way, so it looks as if you're wearing a wreath of mist, with your nose and cheeks all pink. Even though I'm supposed to be seducing you, I admit you look very pretty. I have my hood up, with the visor, to cause water to fall down the front of my face and double the appearance of rain. It's raining."

"That's what I want."

"I mean it's really raining. Let me run out and bring in my stuff. Don't go away," I said.

"Hurry."

The paintings from earlier that afternoon were already pinned upstairs in the hallway. It was only the last one, with water trailing from its oil as if off a duck's back, that I had to bring in, along with the knapsack I used to carry paint, and my collapsible easel.

I picked up the phone again and Julia said, "I'm wet enough. We're going in now. When it rains like this, we might as well be at sea. We just got in and left our boots inside the dining-room door from the garden. Leave the door open. I want to see out. It's cold everywhere, and the good thing is there's a fire I can stand in front of to give me a career, to warm my front until my backside can't stand the cold, and then turn around until my front can't stand it. Everything in the garden is crusted with lichen and crumbling apart. I love the cypress trees you hate, that even the goats can't hurt. You're wrong about those trees. You're wrong about a lot, Nick."

"It's so much work. It's going to be so much work," I said.

"Don't interrupt me," Julia said. "I am raining. It looks, this rain we're having, as if it's come out of Deauville, out of that ocean they have there—which is cloudy, almost milky, and which you walk out into forever and can't get up to your waist, where the grannies and children wade together, the children naked, the old ladies with their black dresses tucked up into the leg elastics of their underpants. I'm in front of the fire and I can't stand how cold it's going to be, getting from the fireplace into the cold bed and those horrible linen sheets."

"No, no," I broke in. "I got the good sheets back. We have the wash-and-wear cotton now. Yvette Turquétil brought them."

"Who's Yvette Turkeywhateveryousaid?"

"A lady who came," I said. "Very nice. Very pretty. What can I say? She turned up, bringing sheets. I had to let her in. I wanted to kiss her all over."

"I thought you were seducing me?"

"Don't you want sheets?"

Julia coughed. "According to an article I read, about now, what with the days getting longer, one of us is supposed to be developing a restless urge to fly thousands of miles and mate. It isn't me."

"It must be me, then," I said.

"Good. Because when you get back, some noises from the basement sound like your cider starting to explode. I'm not going down to look; you'll be here soon enough. Oh, and I mentioned to my mother we were thinking of buying the place in Normandy, and she said, 'Oh, good night!' "

I said, "I have to tell you—"

"Everyone says you're crazy," Julia went on. "Except the men. Then everyone says, 'When can we visit? How can we help?' "

"I did start a responsible list of responsible points to consider responsibly," I said. "But I think I'd better leave it here."

"While we're thinking about it," Julia said, "why don't you bring those shabby, flimsy curtains from the dining room that I always hated, and that ruffle thing off the mantelpiece to keep the dining room from blackening as fast as it wants to with smoke. I'll wash them and see if there's a way to fix them or replace them—I don't know which is worse. . . . Do you still have that duffel bag, the one you used to carry the rugs and bed-spreads and tablecloths to France?"

"I thought I'd travel light, coming home," I said.

Frances and Stellita Stapleton amongst the flock, 1924.

"You may never travel light again. And as long as you're packing the curtains from the dining room, bring those big lined ones
from your mother's bedroom upstairs, the pink ones; they're
impossible, but I might as well see what I can do—while we're
thinking over this idea of yours. . . ."